THE BEST OF THE BIG SOUTH FORK

"If you're headed for the Big South Fork, you couldn't possibly have a better-informed companion.... *The Best of the Big South Fork* gives backpackers, hikers, and explorers the tools they need to travel in some of America's most beautiful backcountry."

—**Dan Coyle, Destinations Editor,** *Outside*

"With the publication of *The Best of the Big South Fork...*, Russ Manning and Sondra Jamieson have moved the Big South Fork National River and Recreation Area into the close-and-accessible category."

—*The Knoxville News-Sentinel*

"... describes hikes in an easy-to-follow manner.... Despite its extensive contents, the book is of size and shape to fit easily into day pack or parka pocket."

—*The Oak Ridger*

"In this book are captured many of these trails..., making the publication a natural for the short trail enthusiasts."

—*Chattanooga News-Free Press*

"Campers and hikers have been quickly snatching up this inexpensive little paperback ... this is a great beginner's guide to a still relatively uncrowded wilderness."

—*The Knoxville Journal*

THE BEST OF THE BIG SOUTH FORK

NATIONAL RIVER AND RECREATION AREA

A Hiker's Guide to Trails and Attractions

A Tag-Along Book
by Russ Manning and
Sondra Jamieson

Second Edition

Laurel Place
Norris, Tenn.

Second Edition; copyright ©1990 by Russ Manning and Sondra Jamieson. First edition, copyright 1989.

All rights reserved.

Printed in the United States of America.

ISBN 0-9625122-4-9

Front Cover: Angel Falls
Back Cover: Yahoo Falls

Published by

> Laurel Place
> P.O. Box 3001
> Norris, TN 37828

Contents

Preface	1
Park History	3
Getting There	6
Geology	8
Human History	10
Plants and Animals	14
Hiking	17

Bandy Creek and Leatherwood Ford

1	Oscar Blevins Farm Loop	22
2	John Litton Farm Loop	25
3	Angel Falls Trail	27
4	Angel Falls Overlook	29
5	Grand Gap Loop	33
6	O&W Bridge	36
7	East Rim and Sunset Overlooks	39
8	Leatherwood Ford Loop	41
9	Dome Rockhouse Trail	43

Middle Creek and Pickett State Park

10	Middle Creek Nature Trail	47
11	Indian Rock House Trail	49
12	Slave Falls Loop	51
13	Charit Creek Lodge Trail	53
14	Twin Arches Trail	56
15	Twin Arches/Charit Creek Loop	59
16	Hazard Cave Loop	62
17	Indian Rockhouse Trail	63
18	Lake Trail Loop	64
19	Hidden Passage Trail	66
20	Buffalo Arch Trail	70

Burnt Mill and Rugby

21	Burnt Mill Bridge Loop	74
22	Honey Creek Loop	77
23	Gentlemen's Swimming Hole and Meeting of the Waters Loop	79
24	Colditz Cove Loop	83

Blue Heron and Yahoo Falls

25	Blue Heron Loop	87
26	Old Tram Road	90
27	Catawba Overlook and Big Spring Falls	92
28	Split Bow Arch Loop	95
29	Bear Creek Overlook	97
30	Yahoo Falls Loop	98
31	Yahoo Arch Trail	100
32	Koger Arch Trail	101

Addresses and Phone Numbers — 102

Acknowledgments

We are grateful to the National Park Service staff for their support in the preparation of this book. Superintendent Bill Dickinson and Park Ranger Management Assistant Ron Wilson provided valuable encouragement during the preparation. Park Ranger Interpreter Howard Ray Duncan and Conley Blevins, Night Security Officer at Blue Heron, gave us the historical perspective, while Tom DesJean, NPS Archeologist, supplied information on the early inhabitants of the region. During our early research of the area, Steve Seven, Chief of Interpretation, served as a resource for general information about the park.

We also thank those who reviewed all or part of our manuscript: Howard Ray Duncan, Ron Wilson, Tom DesJean, Superintendent Dickinson, and Jack Collier, Chief of Resource Management.

The Big South Fork

Preface

Before there was a national river and recreation area, there was the Big South Fork of the Cumberland River.

In the northern part of Tennessee on the Cumberland Plateau, the Clear Fork and New River converged to create the Big South Fork. As the river flowed north to meet the Cumberland River in Kentucky, it plowed a deep canyon, reaching depths of 600 feet in places.

The area that the Big South Fork drains is some of the most primitive and isolated in the eastern U.S. For a time in the early part of the century, dozens of camps and settlements grew up to house the loggers and miners that sought the coal and lumber in the area. With the 1930s Depression, the logging and mining industries began a decline from which they never fully recovered. The camps and settlements were eventually abandoned. Only a few isolated farmsteads and homesites remained. Some coal mining continued, along with oil and gas exploration, but for the most part, the forest and river gorge were left in silence to heal.

Local people who loved the outdoors spent many seasons wandering the forests and exploring the canyons of the Big South Fork watershed. In those days, the Big South Fork was Tennessee's and Kentucky's best kept secret.

Our first encounter was along the road from Oneida that crossed the river at Leatherwood Ford, now TN297. Then it was a gravel road that precariously dipped into the canyon and crossed the old wooden bridge that still spans the river.

From Leatherwood Ford, we explored down river one whole afternoon looking for Angel Falls. We expected a waterfall, but found instead a huge rapids where the water rushed and roiled toward equilibrium.

Exploring the Kentucky portion of the river in search of the more well-known Devils Jump rapids, we wandered through the site of the abandoned Blue Heron Mining Community. Only the old rusting tipple, used to separate the coal, remained as testimony to the large mining operation that once employed over 200 people.

In the southern part of the watershed, near the confluence of the New River and Clear Fork, we drove with friends to Honey Creek Pocket Wilderness, an especially scenic area set aside by the lumber company that still operates in the area. It had rained recently, and the car became mired. We stood in ankle deep mud to push the car to a more firm spot in the road.

And in the northwest, we hiked to Twin Arches at a time when most people thought the possibility of such a phenomenal geologic structure in Tennessee was preposterous. But it wasn't a tall tale, just hard to find. We had to choose the correct jeep trail among many jeep trails off a dirt road; the only designation was a nail in a tree that once held a homemade sign directing you to make the turn.

The threat of eventual development of this isolated area convinced local conservationists that the Big South Fork needed protection before its wilderness character was lost forever. In the 1960s they mounted an effort to protect the river gorge that led to the establishment of the Big South Fork National River and Recreation Area, developed by the Army Corps of Engineers and managed by the National Park Service.

The Big South Fork is still one of our favorite hiking areas. Although it is now tagged with a federal initialism, BSFNRRA, it is still a land of isolated river canyons, natural stone arches, numerous caves, slender waterfalls, and old homesites linked by over a hundred miles of forested trails. In this guide, we describe the best trails and attractions in the Big South Fork and surrounding area.

Norris, Tenn.

Russ Manning and
Sondra Jamieson

Park History

Federal involvement with the Big South Fork dates from 1881, when the Army Corps of Engineers conducted a study for improving navigation on the river. No action was taken.

Then in 1933, the Corps proposed a dam at Devils Jump, a rapids in a narrow part of the river gorge in Kentucky. The dam was originally projected to cost $200 million and would have been the highest dam in the East. Although proposed for Kentucky, the dam would have flooded the river gorge in Tennessee.

During the 1950s and '60s, the Devils Jump Dam was authorized several times in the U. S. Senate but never passed the U.S. House of Representatives. Over the years, other studies recommended flood control lakes, dams at other sites, and pump storage facilities.

In 1966, a local conservation group, the Tennessee Citizens for Wilderness Planning (TCWP), set out to find some kind of permanent protection for the Big South Fork and to put to rest the dam proposals that kept being resurrected. Opposition to the dams was mounted not only to save a pristine area from becoming a lake, but also because the dams were economically insupportable—an independent study showed that only during 11 percent of the year did enough water flow down the river to generate electricity at the proposed Devils Jump Dam.

TCWP first tried to get the Big South Fork included in the Tennessee Scenic Rivers Bill that was soon to pass the State Legislature. But when the bill passed in 1968, the BSF was excluded from the list of rivers.

Then TCWP turned its attention to an impending national bill. An early study by the now-defunct Bureau of Outdoor Recreation had designated the BSF as worthy of being included in a National Wild and Scenic Rivers Bill. But when the national bill was passed, also in 1968, the Big South Fork was again excluded.

Because of the public interest generated by TCWP, Congress then requested new studies on the Big South Fork. One was to examine new dam proposals and a second was to study alternatives. The Corps of Engineers, the Bureau of Outdoor Recreation, and the National Park Service were to be involved in the studies.

TCWP acted as an advisor for the alternatives study, which when made public presented several suggestions for what to do with the Big South Fork, including national recreation area, national forest, national park, and scenic river. With the public sentiment apparently behind saving the river, the decision was made not to bother publishing a dam study.

During this time, TCWP had gained strength by forming a union of various conservation groups, the Big South Fork Coalition. The group was headed by Liane Russell, a research geneticist living in Oak Ridge who along with her husband, Bill Russell, also a research geneticist, helped found TCWP.

The Coalition worked with then Tennessee Senator Howard Baker to draft a bill calling for a combination of national river and recreation area. Introduced in 1972 as part of a water resources bill, the legislation would have automatically given the Army Corps of Engineers authority over the proposed new area. The bill was pocket-vetoed by President Richard Nixon.

During this delay the bill was rewritten so that management of the area would be turned over to the National Park Service after establishment by the Corps of Engineers. Many thought the NPS would bring more experience in preservation and conservation to the task of managing the proposed new national river and recreation area.

The legislation was reintroduced. And in 1974, the Water Resources Development Act was passed authorizing the Big South Fork National River and Recreation Area.

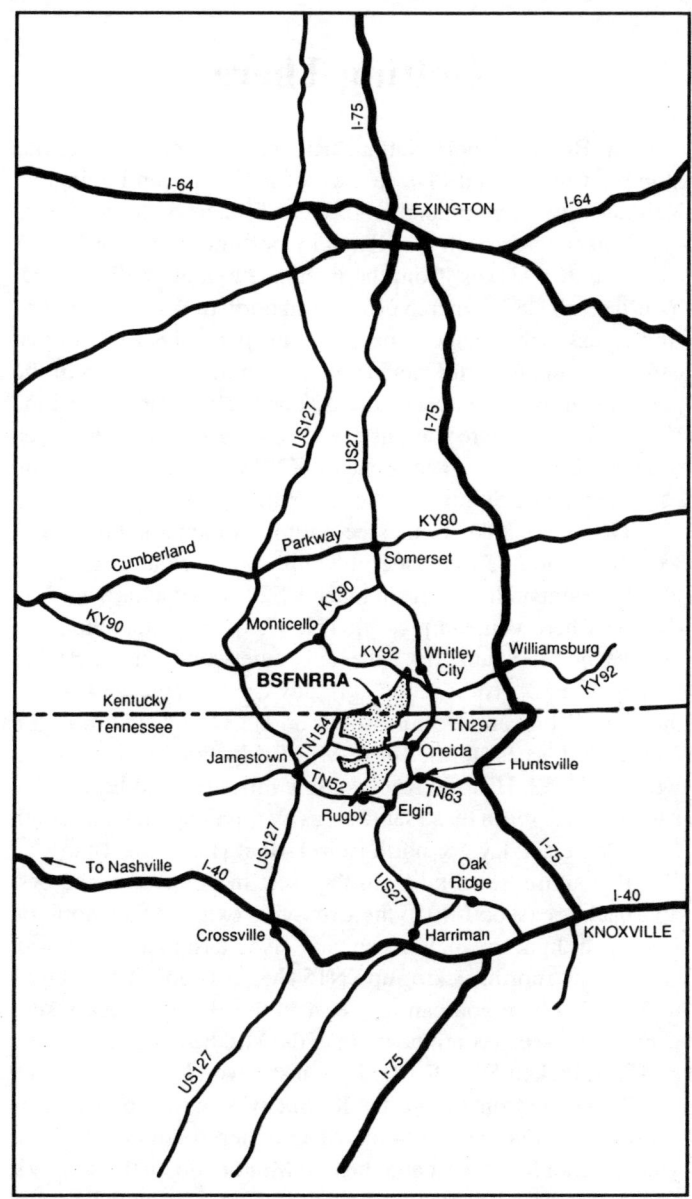

Vicinity Map

Getting There

The Big South Fork National River and Recreation Area lies atop the Cumberland Plateau west of I-75 between Lexington, Kentucky, to the north and Knoxville, Tennessee, to the south.

You can approach the Kentucky portion of the BSFNRRA by taking KY92 west from the interstate exit at Williamsburg. You'll reach US27 where you can turn north to Whitley City and find access to the Yahoo Falls area of the park on KY700, or you can turn south toward Oneida and the Tennessee portion of the park. If you continue west from US27 on KY92, bear right in Pine Knot to Revelo where you can take KY742 to the Blue Heron area of the park, or you can continue on KY92 to Stearns where you can ride the Big South Fork Scenic Railway to Blue Heron.

To approach the Tennessee portion of the park, take TN63 west from the I-75 exit for Huntsville and Oneida. You'll pass through Huntsville and again reach US27; you can turn north to Oneida where you can pick up TN297, which enters the park, crosses the Big South Fork River at Leatherwood Ford, and takes you by the park visitor center at Bandy Creek on the west side of the river. You can also turn south on US27 to TN52 in Elgin. You'll find access to the Burnt Mill Bridge area and, traveling west on TN52, Historic Rugby a few miles beyond Elgin. You can of course reach these same areas by traveling on US27 south from Somerset, Ky., or north from I-40 at Harriman, Tenn.

If you are traveling from the west in Tennessee, the best approach is east on I-40 to the Crossville exit and then north on US127. In Jamestown, you can take TN52 east to Rugby or you can continue north, picking up TN154 headed north. You'll come to TN297 where you can turn east to the Bandy Creek visitor center, or you can continue north to the Middle Creek area of the park and Pickett State Rustic Park just beyond.

Traveling from the west in Kentucky, you can go east on the Cumberland Parkway to Somerset and then south on US27. Or you can take KY90 east and then, in Monticello, pick up KY92, which crosses the Yamacraw Bridge over the Big South Fork and leads to Stearns and the Blue Heron area of the park.

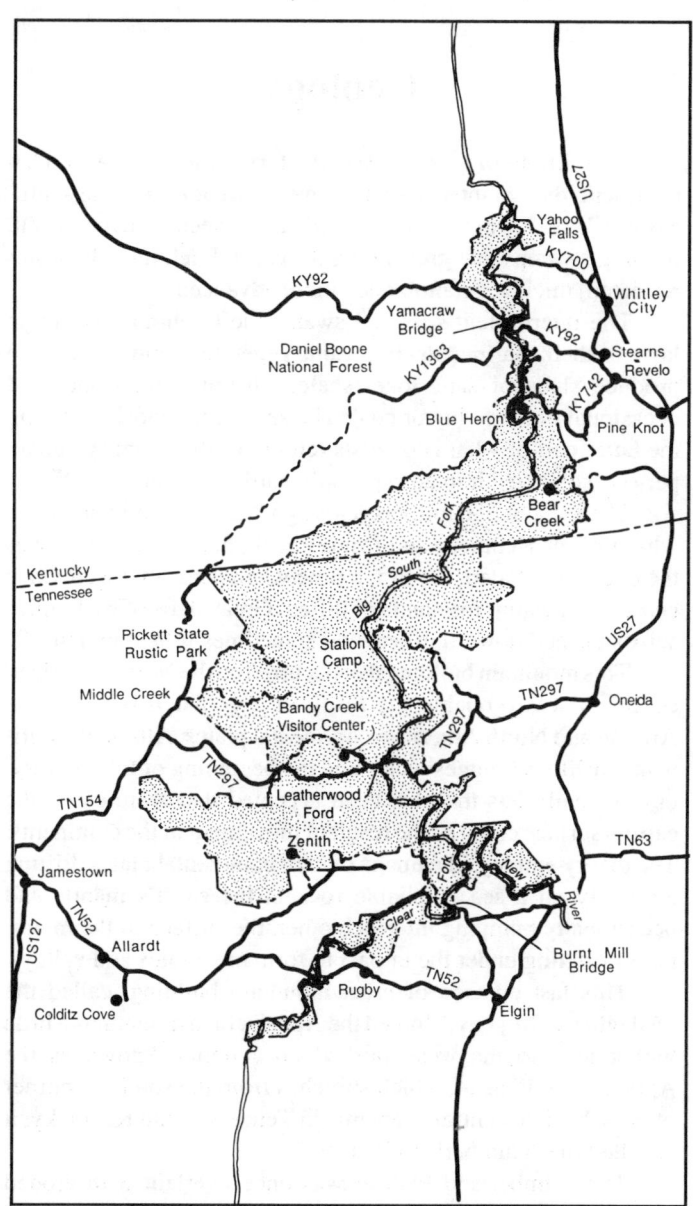

The BSFNRRA

Geology

For millions of years in the prehistory of the North American continent, the sea intermittently covered what is now the southeastern U.S. Each time it invaded, it dropped a layer of silt, burying swamps that grew along the coast. Each time the water retreated, thick vegetation once more advanced.

The intermittent seas and swamps left behind layer upon layer of shell, marine growth, swamp vegetation, and sediment to produce slabs of sandstone, shale, siltstone, limestone, and occasional tiers of clay or coal. The sediment deposited during the latter part of what geologists refer to as the "Pennsylvanian period" solidified into an especially hard sandstone.

Then, about 250 million years ago, the water retreated from what are now Kentucky and Tennessee for the last time. This was the end of the Paleozoic Era, a time when lands that were once beach and swamp rose and solidified. Great slabs of rock miles across pushed upward, tilted, and sometimes folded in half.

This mountain building that occurred on the North American continent was probably the result of a collision between the African and North American continental plates. Although continental drift was suggested around the beginning of this century, only recently has the idea been accepted that features on the earth's surface could be the result of movement of the continents. The theory employs the image of hard continental plates drifting aimlessly on a sea of pliable rock in the earth's mantle and occasionally bumping into each other, the surface of the mountains crinkling under the impact to form mountains and valleys.

This last episode of great mountain building, called the "Allegheny Orogeny," forced the Appalachian mountains a little higher and, to the west, pushed up a region known as the Appalachian Plateau, which stretches from the southern border of New York to central Alabama. In Tennessee and Kentucky, it is called the "Cumberland Plateau."

The Cumberland Plateau was once overlain with eroded beds of soil and silt. These partially remain as the Cumberland Mountains in a region on the northern part of the plateau that experienced greater deformation. But after millions of years of erosion, much of the region is now a plateau 2000 feet above sea level. The plateau was formed due to the layer of hard Pennsylvanian sandstone that resists erosion. Softer rock and dirt washed away, leaving the flat sandstone layer.

Where erosion has taken advantage of a crack in this capstone, a dramatic landscape has resulted. As the Big South Fork flows north across the Cumberland Plateau, it carves a deep canyon, exposing the sandstone layer in the bare rock walls that line the rim. From the canyon edge, it is a 100- to 200-foot drop to the forest and rubble zone that slopes steeply to the edge of the river in the center of the gorge.

Where side streams flow over breaks in the sandstone, they quickly scoop out softer layers below, forming waterfalls. Because of the hard sandstone, the lip of a waterfall refuses to break off, and so as softer layers behind the waterfall are washed away, a natural amphitheater is formed, which is why you can walk behind many waterfalls on the plateau.

As groundwater dissolves limestone layers beneath the sandstone, many caves appear. Because surface erosion proceeds faster, the surrounding landscape has been lowered, and the openings to these caves now usually appear as gaping holes in rock walls.

In exposed hillsides and ridges, erosion sweeps away soft layers under the hard sandstone, creating numerous stone arches. The process might be by headward erosion, in which a gully erodes up a slope, eventually breaking through the ridge to create the arch. In other cases, headward erosion or the effect of gravity forms a cavity in a ridge while a joint cutting across the cavity is widened by erosion to separate the top of the opening from the ridgeline.

All these geologic features—steep-walled canyons, high waterfalls, gaping caves, and massive arches—make the Big South Fork one of the most interesting areas for hiking in the eastern U.S.

Human History

The upper Cumberland area that encompasses the Big South Fork was originally occupied by a succession of native American peoples, from the Paleo-Indians, through the Archaic and Woodland cultures, to the Mississippian tradition.

These early inhabitants were originally big game hunters. By about 1000 BC, they had developed pottery and led a more refined transitional existence, living along the rivers when the walleye were running and shellfish could be had, and in season, living in the numerous rock shelters in the forests where they could easily gather hickory nuts and chestnuts to supplement the game they killed. Around 900 AD, they began to grow some of their food and, by 1000 AD, were experienced horticulturists with corn and squash a primary part of their diet. This led the people to move to the broad, fertile river valleys away from the plateau country, which because of the topography and the marginal soil, was not very good for growing crops.

By the time whitemen encountered the American Indians of the southeastern United States, they had coalesced into the historic tribes—the Cherokees, Creeks, Chickasaws, and Shawnees among them. The Cherokees and Shawnees dominated the region; the Cherokees in Tennessee, Georgia, and the Carolinas and the Shawnees in Kentucky along the Ohio River. Although both tribes claimed the plateau as their hunting grounds, archeological studies in the park have uncovered little evidence that can be directly related to these historic tribes. Most of the discovered relics date from the early Indian cultures that actually lived in the area. The Cherokees and Shawnees did not live on the plateau but rather considered it a sort of a no-man's-land between the two traditionally warring tribes.

Hunting parties from both sides made frequent forays into the area along with occasional groups of Chickasaws and Creeks. Fighting probably ensued whenever they encountered each other. The hunters intermittently used the traditional rock shelters as camps, but apparently left behind few artifacts since definitive evidence of their presence in the Big South Fork is still being sought.

The Indians lost their claim to the Southeast region, including the Cumberland Plateau, in several treaties forced on them in the late-1700s and early 1800s. At about this time, long hunters began penetrating the region. They and their descendents eventually settled the Big South Fork, taking up subsistence farming. The Blevins, Slaven, and Phillips families are descendents of some of these early long hunters.

The original settlers, which included Revolutionary War veterans compensated with land grants in the area, first lived in the rock shelters the Indians had frequented, closing them off with leaning poles. They soon built pole cabins with mud floors. Over the next 50 years, the floor was covered by split-log flooring, the walls became thick hewn logs, a loft or second story was placed on the ground-level structure, and a stone chimney was added. They cleared land for crops and livestock and continued to add wild game to their diet.

Archeological evidence indicates that during the period from about 1812 to 1865 much saltpeter mining occurred. An ingredient in gunpowder, the saltpeter was a precious commodity during the War of 1812 and the Civil War. The "niter," as it was called, was sent to powder mills in Lexington, Ky., where it was mixed with the sulfur and charcoal necessary to make gunpowder.

Coal mining and lumbering gradually became important economic activities, contributing to a steady increase in population. The last group of immigrants were the managers and workers needed to run the railroads, coal mines, and lumbering operations of a large industrial development that occurred between 1900 and 1920. The largest operation was the Stearns Coal and Lumber Company founded in 1902, which eventually commanded many thousands of acres of land. In its peak year, the Stearns Company produced 970,000 tons of coal and 18,000,000 board feet of lumber.

With the Depression of the 1930s, the economic prospects of the region declined, never to recover. The coal company towns, the lumber mills, and rail lines were abandoned. Stearns opened its Blue Heron Mine in 1937, still hoping to bolster its operations.

Although the mine continued operation until 1962, the end of the economic boom had already been determined.

By the time the national river and recreation area was authorized in 1974, there were only about forty households of year-round residents still living within the proposed boundaries, primarily on subsistence farms that occasionally included a fenced-off rock shelter as a holding area for livestock.

The rock shelters, or "rockhouses" as they are often called, played a primary role in the human history of the Big South Fork area. It is in these shelters that most of the archeological work is being carried out. Not only do these natural shelters preserve the remaining artifacts of the native peoples that lived here and the settlers that first came to the area, they are storehouses of the environmental record of the last 1000-9000 years. Because of the shelters' dryness, such natural artifacts as pollen and bone remain to give evidence of past flora and fauna and the climatic changes the region has experienced.

When you are passing through these areas on the hikes we describe in this guide, leave them undisturbed. Digging and rummaging around in the shelters destroys the archeological record, making it impossible to piece together the history of the Big South Fork region. When people loot the area, they are not just taking artifacts; they are stealing the past.

Clara Sue Blevins House Historic Site

Plants and Animals

At one time the Cumberland Plateau was covered by a mixed mesophytic forest, a complex association in which several tree species are dominant. Little of this original forest remains today. But within the numerous canyons of the plateau, remnants of the forest can still be found. The Big South Fork flows through such a mixed mesophytic forest, the extreme diversity resulting from a varied topography and thus varied habitat.

The canopy layer consists of beech, sugar maple, red oak, tuliptree (or yellow poplar), white oak, basswood, sweet buckeye, and hemlock. Also abundant are birch, black cherry, white ash, red maple, and umbrella and cucumber magnolias. Along the streams grow willow, sycamore, sweet gum, and river birch. Where lumbering and erosion have scarred the forest, oak and hickory have become the dominant trees and Virginia pine grows on slopes where white oak and beech once flourished.

The understory is dogwood, hop hornbeam, sourwood, striped maple, holly, redbud, ironwood, serviceberry, and sassafras. Rhododendron is the dominant shrub, with frequent mountain laurel and occasional azalea. Mayapple and a variety of ferns gather on the forest floor, and the ground is scattered with showy flowers, including trillium, violets, delphinium, phacelia, phlox, bloodroot, spring beauty, fire pink, wild iris, anemone, and in late summer and fall, asters and goldenrods.

Not all plant species occur in any one area. Distinct climax communities have developed in which only some of these species are present, although the communities are actually part of one climax forest. The segregation of tree associations is the result of differences in elevation, slope exposure, and moisture. From a perch on the edge of the river canyon, thickets of pine, chestnut oak, sourwood, and various shrubs begin a progression of forest communities as the canyon walls descend and reach the river's edge.

The mixed pine forest on the rim of the canyon is patrolled by white-tailed deer. The pine warbler and red-breasted nuthatch forage for conifer seeds and insects. Hawks and crows nest in the trees. In the mixed pine-hardwood habitats, hairy woodpeckers, common flickers, and pileated woodpeckers search the trees for insects. The pine seeds are food for the red crossbill, evening grosbeak, bobwhite, turkey, gray squirrel, eastern chipmunk, and white-footed mouse. The eastern cottontail frequents areas where foliage is near the ground.

The massive walls of the canyon stand bare except for a few irregularities in the rock surface that provide footholds for alum root, a few ferns, and small wind-swept pines. Vultures, kingfishers, and swallows nest in precarious crevices in the cliff face, and an occasional bat clings to the underside of a rock overhang. The red-tailed hawk surveys the canyon from a perch, and the timber rattlesnake and northern copperhead bask in the bright sun.

From the base of the walls, the south-facing slopes descend, clothed in mixed oak communities where turkey, gray squirrel, and opossum are attracted to the mast and thick undergrowth. The wood thrush, hooded warbler, and downy woodpecker frequent the understory, while the red-eyed vireo, scarlet tanager, and tufted-titmouse feed in the canopy.

In the shaded coves of the north-facing slopes, where understory and groundcover are inhibited, hemlock and rhododendron live in virtual solitude except for a passing deer, bobcat, or fox. Pine and blackpole warblers and the golden-crowned kinglet search for seeds and insects in the canopy.

A forest of sugar maple, beech, and yellow birch on the low moist slopes is a refuge for gray fox, skunk, and raccoon. The barred owl and red-shouldered hawk search for the smoky shrew, eastern mole, eastern woodrat, white-footed mouse, and eastern chipmunk.

Along the floor of the canyon persists an alluvial forest of sycamore and river birch with wild oats and dense stands of cane; beaver and muskrat, maybe even mink and otter, live in synchronization with the river. The Louisiana waterthrush, spotted sandpiper, and American woodcock explore the wet sand.

A gravel and rubble zone possessing a few shrubs edges the river. The strip is inhabited by the bullfrog, southern leopard frog, pickerel frog, water snake, and midland painted turtle. Deer and other large species come to the stream for water as wood ducks paddle by.

The river breathes with its rapids and riffles, giving life to the riverweed growing on the flooded rocks with diatoms and algae in association. These support the zooplankton and aquatic insects that are food for the bluebreast darter, rainbow trout, longear sunfish, and smallmouth bass. Belted kingfishers skim the surface, and green herons lunge for fish and amphibians. Rough-winged swallows, eastern phoebes, and bats feed on the congregating insects.

Recent floods leave debris hanging in the limbs of shrubs and trees along the riverbank. Small ponds left by the retreating waters and replenished by rains are filled with life in spring. Salamanders and turtles grope through the cattails, rushes, and occasional peat moss of the larger waterholes. Swallows and eastern bluebirds flit across the ponds as they feed on the numerous insects attracted to the water. Puddles serve as nurseries for amphibians that hurry toward maturity before the warming summer sun dries the pools to dusty bowls on the forest floor.

From the overlook of the canyon, the different communities meld into one, and what appears is not distinct boundaries but a wholeness and a balance that can be achieved only by undisturbed nature.

Hiking

The best ways to see the Big South Fork National River and Recreation Area are on foot, on horse, and by canoe or raft. While the last two ways have their special attractions, hiking is the one form of recreation that can be enjoyed by most everyone. The favorite times to hike the Big South Fork are spring and fall, when the temperatures are mild and you have the special attraction of abundant wildflowers or a forest of red and gold.

The hikes we describe in this guide range from short walks to long trails that may be used for backpacking. The accompanying maps are designed to help you in finding the trails. The trail numbers correspond to the numbers on the maps. Once at the trailheads, you should have little trouble finding your way while hiking, using our descriptions and the signs along the trails. But if you want more detailed maps of the terrain you are covering, you'll need to get topographical maps of the area from your local map supplier or check with the park visitor center.

For each of the hikes in this book, we have rated the trails easy, moderate, or difficult. This rating is based on the strenuousness of the trail, how much up and down there is. As a result, while a 10-mile trail would be difficult for someone not used to hiking, it might be rated easy if it is relatively level. So if you are not accustomed to hiking, look not only at the degree of difficulty, but also at the distance you will walk (double that if the description says "one way") and notice the precautions you will have to take at stream and boulder crossings or steep bluffs.

We have based the difficulty of each trail on the ability of an average person, someone who hikes occasionally but for whom a walk ascending several hundred feet is not a daily occurrence. So more experienced hikers may find many of the moderate hikes easy and the difficult hikes moderate. Someone who rarely hikes may find the easy and moderate trails to be difficult.

The elevation change we give for each trail indicates a difference in elevation between its highest and lowest point. But there could be several ups and downs; so while walking a trail that gains 500 feet, you could ascend and descend a total of many more feet. At times, we say a trail is level because there is no appreciable loss or gain, but of course no trail is really level and you'll find the trail undulating across the terrain.

For those of you who wish to walk farther than the trails described, we have also included trail connections so you may combine several trails for a longer walk. Many of the trails we include here are merely the beginning of long trails that cross the park and can be used for hikes of more than one day.

All the hiking trails in the Big South Fork are marked with a red arrow in a white blaze, with the exceptions of the John Muir Trail, which has a blue silhouette of Muir on a white blaze, the Sheltowee Trace, which has a white turtle, and the Yahoo Falls trails, which have several colors. The blazes are usually spaced close enough that you will see one ahead whenever you begin to wonder if you have strayed from the trail.

Even if you are out for only a short walk, you should wear walking shoes or hiking boots, which are designed to give sure footing and to support ankles. For day hikes in which you intend to be out more than an hour or two, carry along water, snacks, and rain gear; it rains frequently in the Big South Fork, especially in the winter and spring. You should also take along a first aid kit and a map and compass; and just in case you get lost, bring along extra clothes, a flashlight, and matches for starting a fire. If you are backpacking, you of course need everything for surviving in the open overnight and for however many days you choose to be out. If you are inexperienced in backpacking, the park rangers or your local outfitters can give advice on the equipment needed.

If you plan to camp in the backcountry, let a ranger know your plans, even though registration is not required. You may camp anywhere in the backcountry, but set up at least 25 feet from trails, rock shelters, and major geologic and historic features and at least 100 feet from roads and parking areas. You may use down timber for campfires.

While you are out there, take care of the park. Don't pick the wildflowers and leave historic and archeological areas undisturbed; digging for Indian relics is not allowed.

Take care of yourself as well; be especially careful climbing on rocks and walking along the edge of the river or along the edge of the gorge. We mention such situations in the trail descriptions, but we cannot mention every place where you should be careful. So we expect you to take responsibility for your own safety, keeping in mind that hiking in a wilderness setting far from medical attention is an inherently hazardous activity.

Water in the backcountry should be considered contaminated. Boil all water a few minutes before drinking to destroy bacteria and other microorganisms, including Giardia, a protozoan causing an intestinal disorder called "Giardiasis."

The Big South Fork does have snakes, including the northern copperhead and the timber rattler. To be safe, simply watch where you put your feet, and if you must walk through high brush and weeds, explore ahead with a stick. We have encountered several snakes in our years of hiking the Big South Fork, but have yet to see one of the poisonous species. If you do encounter snakes, leave them alone; they belong here.

During the warm spring and summer days, the gnats and mosquitoes can be a bother. We have seen more than our share of these. You might carry along insect repellant for when the gnats become incessant. But only occasionally do they get that bad.

Before starting off on a hike, you might spray your shoetops, socks, and pants with repellant to discourage ticks, one type of which, the deer tick, can transmit a spirochete that causes Lyme disease. Although Lyme disease is still rare in the southeastern states, you should remain very conscious of keeping ticks off you and checking for ticks after a hike.

And there is poison ivy. If you stay to the trails, you'll probably not contact any. But if you do venture off trail or encounter an overgrown trail, watch for the three-leaf clusters.

Finally, hunting is allowed in the park, subject to the regulations of the States of Kentucky and Tennessee. Check at the visitor center or with any ranger to find out whether hunting is currently going on and if there are any areas you should avoid.

Don't be discouraged from walking the trails by all these warnings. The Big South Fork is well worth having to take a few precautions. With only a little effort, you'll see canyons, caves, forests, waterfalls, old homesteads, sandstone arches, wildflowers, birds, mammals, and if you get far enough off the main thoroughfares, only an occasional Homo sapiens.

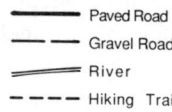

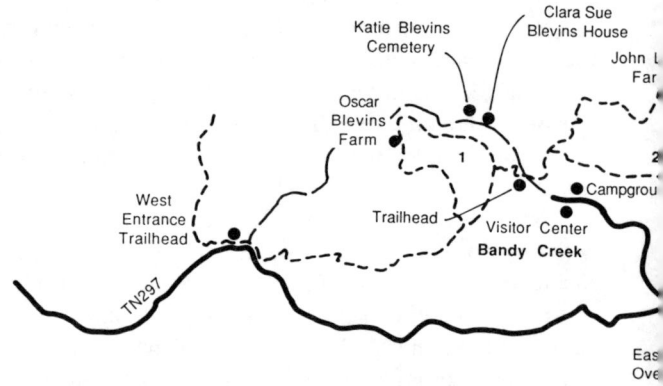

Bandy Creek and Leatherwood Ford

1 Oscar Blevins Farm Loop

3.4 miles
Easy
Elevation change: 200 ft.
Cautions: Creek crossings, stairs
Connections: West Entrance

Attractions: Stands of tall laurel and rhododendron line the trail along Bandy Creek on the way to the Oscar Blevins Farm Historic Site.

Trailhead: Turn north on the Bandy Creek Road off TN297 west of Leatherwood Ford and go 2.2 miles, past the visitor center on the left, to the end of the pavement. Parking for the Bandy Creek Trailhead is on the left.

Description: From the trailhead, walk 0.2 mile to get to the Oscar Blevins Farm Loop. This connecting trail begins as a gravel path among young pines and thickets of blackberries. You'll cross a horse trail at 0.1 mile. Just before encountering the loop, you'll cross a creek on a footbridge. From the sign at the loop, you can go left or right to get to the Blevins Farm. The best approach is to hike the loop clockwise.

The trail descends gradually following the small creek you crossed earlier. Very soon you'll find yourself in a miniature gorge with the creek cascading down the rock bluff and spilling over a small waterfall just at a wooden platform where you must walk down a wooden stairway. For the next 0.8 mile, the trail passes through stands of laurel and crosses side creeks on stepping stones and boardwalks, following along a rock bluff on the right. At one point the trail takes you under an overhang and behind a small waterfall trickling off the rock ledge. At a mile, you'll cross Bandy Creek on a bridge and encounter the turnoff for the West Entrance that's in 2.4 miles. Bear right to continue on the loop.

1890s Farmhouse

The trail soon merges with an old roadbed, with fencing and once-cleared fields on the left and towering laurel on the right. Along the road, you'll find an old housesite with a chicken coop on the right. The trail descends, crossing a small stream, and soon joins Bandy Creek on the right tucked into a forest floor of rhododendron, laurel, and hemlock. At 1.5 miles the trail bears left, soon to cross Bandy Creek.

A split rail fence signals your arrival at the Oscar Blevins Farm, as do the remains of the outhouse and springhouse on the trail's left. The panoramic view across the open field centers on a large barn flanked by a hog shed, chicken coop, corn crib, log house, and another shed beside a more modern frame house. The farm, a unique historic site representative of early 20th century homesteads in the region, was the home of Oscar and Martha Ermon Blevins. Oscar built the frame house in a style unique to the area, called the "Cumberland House." The characteristic layout is one and a half stories, two rooms wide and two rooms deep, a central chimney, and two front doors with a long front porch. The houses are wood frame construction, typically clapboard or covered with rolled asphalt.

The older log house on the farm was built in the 1890s by an uncle of Oscar Blevins. The Park Service intends to preserve the farm with its significant structures as an historic site.

Oscar Blevins is buried in the Katie Blevins Cemetery next to the Clara Sue Blevins House Historic Site. You can reach the cemetery and historic site by continuing west on the gravel road that is a continuation of the road that passes the Bandy Creek Trailhead.

In front of the Oscar Blevins' home, turn right on a footpath. The next 1.4 miles back to the beginning of the loop, you'll pass through hemlock forests and carpets of ferns and cross several boardwalks and bridges over streams.

2 John Litton Farm Loop

5.9 miles
Moderate
Elevation change: 200 ft.
Cautions: Ladders, creek crossings
Connections: Grand Gap Loop

Attractions: This loop takes you by terraced rock bluffs and Fall Branch Falls en route to the John Litton Farmstead.

Trailhead: Follow the directions in Trail #1 to the Bandy Creek Trailhead. Take a 0.4-mile path to the right to get to the Farm Loop. You'll cross the road at the end of the pavement and pass behind the swimming pool to the loop's beginning. An alternative is to park at the pool, which is across from the visitor center.

Description: You can go left 2.2 miles or right 3.7 miles to the Litton Farm. Turn right for the best approach. The trail begins as a gravel path that parallels a gravel road on the left for a time, then swings right and crosses a stream on wooden planks before leading into a fragrant pine and laurel forest.

Soon you'll hear Fall Branch as the trail switches back and drops toward the creek to your right. You will skirt sandstone shelves on your left with hemlocks balanced at the edge. Wooden ladders and switchbacks take you past dripping rock overhangs and gradually drop you into a carpet of ferns alongside the creek.

You'll pass by rock bluffs and make several stream crossings over wooden bridges. You will encounter the state forest boundary and then a power line. At 2.0 miles you'll come to Fall Branch Falls. The creek pours off a rock shelf and drops approximately ten feet into a green pool—a perfect spot for lunch, relaxing, or maybe even a splash in the pool.

From here the trail climbs away from Fall Branch through a young pine grove to the North Fork of Fall Branch. Along the way, watch for climbing fern, so thick at one location on both sides of the trail it reminded us of kudzu.

Take the bridge across the North Fork, and at about 3 miles you'll come to a junction. If you go straight, you will reach the Grand Gap Loop in 1.9 miles. Bear left. Crisscross the creek over plank bridges, watching for lady's-slipper orchids in the spring, until the trail merges with an old roadbed leading to the farm.

The farmstead sits in a cove to the left. You first see an old shed where in spring you're greeted by blooming iris. Downhill from the shed is the house John Litton built in 1901. He was known as a master cabin builder and built several in the park, including the John Litton Cabin on Parch Corn Creek in the late 1880s. Litton died in 1935 and is buried with his wife Elvira in the Katie Blevins Cemetery next to the Clara Sue Blevins House Historic Site at Bandy Creek.

The Litton Farm is also referred to as the "General Slaven Farm." "General" was his name, not a military title. The Slavens were the only other family to live here; they added a frame addition to the original cabin.

The trail curves left over an earthen dam holding back blackberry bushes and a stream-fed pond still alive with fish. Above the pond are some rockhouses once enclosed with wooden rails where the families kept livestock. The trail then joins an old road that leads to a barn. The style is a side-opening English barn, where the drivethrough is on the side instead of the gable end.

Just to the right of the barn a trail sign sends you away from the road, skirting the farm's boundary. You'll cross a bridge and switchback right, climbing away from the farm. The ascent includes several more switchbacks and a set of stairs.

At about 4.5 miles the trail joins a roadbed leading to a clearing and homesite. Cross the clearing for 100 yards then turn right, walking along the rim of a grassy bowl for another 200 yards. Watch for deer at a pond off to the left across the meadow. At the end of the clearing at 4.7 miles, the trail turns left on a gravel road at a sign sending you the last mile back.

You'll encounter a horse trail to the right at 5.6 miles that is an alternative way back to the Bandy Creek Trailhead. The sign there says it's a mile to the campground, but you'll only be going half a mile. You'll pass through woods and then emerge into an open area where you'll turn left, cross the gravel road, and turn left again when you intersect the Oscar Blevins Farm Loop trail.

③ Angel Falls Trail

2.0 miles one way
Easy
Level
Cautions: Creek crossings
Connections: John Hawk's Place, Station Camp

Attractions: Along this river trail featuring rock bluffs and a view of Angel Falls, you'll enjoy wildflowers in the spring.

Trailhead: From the junction of Bandy Creek Road and TN297 go east on TN297 one mile, or from the park's east entrance sign drive west 2.2 miles, to the Leatherwood Ford River Access and the Leatherwood Ford Trailhead.

Description: You'll find at this river access several boardwalks along the river's edge. They have been built so low to the water that they are often submerged when the river is at flood stage. So as you enjoy a boardwalk vantage point from which to view the river, you might find a log washed up from the river sitting on a bench.

To begin the trail to Angel Falls, walk to the north end of the parking area and look for a jeep road blocked by a gate. This is the trailhead, marked by a sign for Angel Falls.

With the Big South Fork River on your left, stroll through the shade of hemlocks, rhododendron, and mixed hardwood. Occasionally you'll cross side streams making their way to the river from rock bluffs on your right. In spring a garden of wild iris, columbine, trillium, geranium, and more line your way. At about one mile, look off to your right as you cross a wooden bridge for a glimpse of a reclaimed coal mine.

At 1.8 miles a small trail to the left leads to the river then rejoins the main trail. This is the access to the portage around Angel Falls. Unless you want to go down to the river's edge at this point, keep straight ahead. Soon you'll pass alongside a rock overhang on the right and just ahead on the left will be a wooden deck overlooking Angel Falls.

What you'll find is a huge rapids formed by boulders standing in the river. The rapids are all that's left of a low waterfall that was dynamited in the 1950s, probably by fishermen hoping to improve navigation on the river. There was little improvement.

Although the falls is no longer a waterfall, it's still an impressive sight, a churning sluice of water that rushes downstream. Legend has it that Angel Falls was given its name to counter the Devils Jump rapids that's downstream in the northern section of the park near Blue Heron.

For a view of the rapids from the river's edge, take the trail down toward the river. At the end of this trail you'll be at the river, but downstream from the rapids. For a better approach, watch for a small path off to the left on the other side of a log beside the trail. That path drops you to the river's edge near the rapids. The view of the canyon while standing on the rocks that form the rapids makes the climb down worthwhile.

You must use caution here. If you slip on the rocks and fall in the water, the swift current will sling you against boulders and perhaps trap you underwater. People have died here.

From Angel Falls, you can continue on the main trail 1.3 miles to John Hawk's Place. There's not much there to mark the spot of the cabin that was abandoned by John "Hawk" Smith in the 1940s. You'd have to know where to look to find remains of the foundation. This is sometimes referred to as the John Hawk Mine Site because it is thought by some that he operated a mine here. From the John Hawk Place, the trail eventually goes all the way to Station Camp in about 5 miles.

If you are not continuing on, return along the same path to the Leatherwood Ford Trailhead.

4 Angel Falls Overlook

3.0 miles one way
Difficult
Elevation gain: 500 ft.
Cautions: Stream crossings, steep ascent, boulder passages,
narrow ledge crossing, ladder
Connections: Grand Gap Loop

Attractions: This trail takes you along the river, past rushing streams, through boulder passages, and atop the plateau for one of the best views of the Big South Fork gorge.

Trailhead: Follow the directions in Trail #3 to the Leatherwood Ford Trailhead.

Description: To begin the overlook trail, walk across the old Leatherwood Ford Bridge and climb the stairs into the woods. Turn right at the trail sign towards Fall Branch. If there has been a recent rain, the old bridge may be underwater; in that case you'll have to walk across the highway bridge to get across the river and turn right into the woods.

The trail you are on is actually the John Muir Trail, a national historic trail that commemorates the 1867 journey through the Cumberlands by the noted conservationist and founder of the Sierra Club. Although Muir became famous wandering the Sierras in California, the Cumberlands were the first mountains he ever saw. The trail is blazed by a blue silhouette of John Muir.

With rock bluffs on your left laced with laurel blossoms in May and the river drifting below on your right, you will encounter several side streams, cascades, and foot bridges as you meander through a hemlock and mixed-hardwood forest. This part of the trail is a wonderland of wildflowers in spring. You'll see crested dwarf iris, bluets, cinquefoil, penstemon, fire pink, geranium, purple phacelia, foamflower, may apple, marsh blue violets, trillium, bloodroot, dwarf dandelion, and more.

Fall Branch Bridge

If you are just out for a stroll, this first part of the trail is an easy walk and a good one in spring.

At about 1.8 miles you'll begin paralleling Fall Branch upstream from where it joins the Big South Fork. At 2.0 miles the trail crosses a curved bridge over Fall Branch, which roars and rushes through boulders as it hurries to the river. On the other side, you'll walk downstream with a rock bluff on your left and the stream on your right before you make a switchback up.

The remainder of the trail is a continuous climb with switchbacks, stone steps, and boulder passages. Twice the trail runs into a large boulder; in both cases bear left. The trail then levels off for a time with a rock bluff on your right and the valley of Fall Branch on your left. The trail passes under a rock overhang and crosses a wet-weather stream.

Then, at about 2.6 miles, you'll switchback onto a rock shelf as the trail leads into a small gorge created by the stream you just crossed. Notice the iron deposits in the rock face along the ledge. Climb the ladder and follow the trail as it ascends through a hemlock and rhododendron cove sandwiched between canyon walls. Toward the upper end you will pass some large beech trees.

When you arrive at the top at 2.8 miles, the trail connects with the Grand Gap Loop. Turn right to get to the Angel Falls Overlook for a grand view of the river in another 0.2 mile.

You must continue along the Grand Gap Loop a few paces past the first overlook to actually get a view of Angel Falls below. But the first overlook is the best with the river sweeping by vertical rock walls. This view's only competition for best view in the park is the sight from the Bear Creek Overlook to the north.

Retracing your steps, you'll have a total hike of 6 miles.

Angel Falls Overlook

5 Grand Gap Loop

6.8 miles
Easy
Elevation change: 100 ft.
Cautions: High bluffs
Connections: John Muir Trail, John Litton Farm Loop

Attractions: This loop offers spectacular views of the Big South Fork and Angel Falls.

Trailhead: Follow the directions in Trail #3 to the Leatherwood Ford Trailhead and walk Trail #4 to the Angel Falls Overlook.

Description: After walking 2.8 miles to get to the Grand Gap Loop, you can turn either right or left to hike the 6.8-mile loop. Either route is a continuation of the John Muir Trail.

Turn right to get to Angel Falls Overlook. The trail continues past the main overlook, paralleling the gorge rim past other views where you can actually see Angel Falls far below.

The rest of the trail for most of the loop periodically swings away from the edge then returns, remaining relatively level with only a few ups and downs. You'll be passing through the typical pine and mixed hardwood forest of the plateautop. In spring, you'll see occasional yellow stargrass and violet wood-sorrel.

The trail swings away from the bluff edge. In about 0.4 mile, you'll follow a rock bluff on the left and come to a moss-capped arch, about 8 feet high and 50 feet long. Soon after, the trail passes by a rock overhang.

At about one mile, watch for the trail to make a sharp switchback right. The trail appears to go straight because most people have missed the turn and created a path straight ahead. If you miss it too, you'll find the trail just disappears; retrace your steps, and you'll see the trail headed downhill. You'll switchback down to the bluff edge, where a short path takes you to a narrow promontory that thrusts you out for a wide-angle view of Angel Falls upstream. This overlook is well worth the walk.

You'll soon turn away from the gorge. At 1.4 miles the trail crosses a little footbridge over a seep that comes from under a rock overhang. Later, the trail enters a hemlock woods at 1.9 miles and joins an old roadbed at 2.1 miles at Grand Gap. The name is one given to the area by the Corps of Engineers.

Turn right on the roadbed, and then in a few yards the trail turns left off the road. You'll pass another rock overhang at 2.2 miles and then top out on a bluff at 2.4 miles. The trail then switchbacks left and climbs up and over a small ridge. The last time we hiked this trail, this next section had several down trees that made quite an obstacle course for us to get through.

At 3.1 miles the trail again joins an old roadbed. Turn right, and in a few yards the trail turns left away from the road. At 3.7 miles the trail comes to a bluff overlooking a tributary canyon of the Big South Fork. Massive stone walls stand across the way. The trail soon rejoins the old roadbed; then it swings right from the road to an overlook of where this side canyon joins the river.

The trail then rejoins the road, ascends slightly, crosses another old roadbed at 4.0 miles, and then again at 4.4 miles. At 5.2 miles the trail loops around an open area that was once the homesite of Alfred and Elva Smith. Alfred was a logger for the Stearns Coal and Lumber Company. When the lumbering operations were discontinued in the 1940s, the Smiths had to leave their plateau retreat. They left behind their son Archie, who was only four months old when he died of pneumonia in 1932. His grave is at 6.1 miles along the trail.

But before that, you'll reach a junction at 5.5 miles with the John Muir Trail turning right and continuing north; Station Camp Creek is in 10.4 miles. Turn left to complete the Grand Gap Loop. You'll cross an old road at 5.6 miles and come to the connector to the John Litton Farm Loop on the right. You can reach the loop in 1.9 miles and walk to Bandy Creek Campground in 4.9 miles.

Continuing on, you'll reach the valley of Fall Branch at about 6.6 miles on the right. You'll have a broad sandstone bluff from which to view where Fall Branch joins the Big South Fork at 6.7 miles. You'll then parallel on the right the small canyon that contains the trail down to Leatherwood Ford and complete the loop at 6.8 miles. You then must return along the trail to Leatherwood Ford. The total hiking distance is 12.4 miles.

Angel Falls from Grand Gap Loop

⑥ O&W Bridge

2.3 miles one way
Moderate
Elevation gain: 100 ft.
Cautions: Creek crossings, short steep ascent
Connections: Leatherwood Ford Loop

Attractions: Enjoy river and bluff views along this trail to the O&W Railroad trestle. Wildflowers are plentiful in the spring.

Trailhead: Follow the directions in Trail #3 to the Leatherwood Ford Trailhead.

Description: Walk south under the Leatherwood Ford Bridge to a trail junction sign. If you climb the rock steps on your left to the bridge above, you'll be on the Leatherwood Ford Loop. To reach the O&W Bridge, follow the trail leading straight into the woods; this is the John Muir National Historic Trail, blazed by a silhouette of John Muir.

The John Muir Trail connects with the Sheltowee Trace National Recreation Trail to the north that descends through Daniel Boone National Forest in Kentucky and passes through the northern part of the BSFNRRA. "Sheltowee" is the Shawnee word for "turtle" and was the name the Indians gave to Daniel Boone. To the southeast, the John Muir Trail will eventually connect with the Appalachian Trail when construction is complete through Tennessee.

Walking along the river, on your right, you'll cross wooden bridges and meander through a fern and wildflower gathering and boulder displays. This section of the trail is actually part of the Leatherwood Ford Loop Trail. At 0.5 mile you will encounter a junction, where the loop turns left switching back up the steep bank. Continue straight ahead until at about 0.7 mile you begin a climb up the bluff on rock steps and switchbacks.

Walk along the bluff's edge until the trail joins an old roadbed to descend to a stream crossing. The trail then follows a

O&W Bridge

stream on your left through a hemlock canopy before allowing you a view of the bridge through the woods to your right.

The Oneida and Western Railroad Bridge was a link in the now-abandoned O&W Railroad that connected Oneida with Jamestown to the west. The O&W Trestle was erected in 1915 and abandoned in 1954. The bridge is of the Whipple Truss design, manufactured between 1847 and 1900. It was once used on another railroad but was brought here and adapted for use by the O&W. Very few Whipple Truss bridges survive today.

To the east, the old railbed is now a dirt road out of Verdun off TN297 that can be negotiated by cars. The section of abandoned railbed west of the bridge is a muddy stretch that leads to the Zenith area and that only four-wheel drives and all-terrain bicycles can handle. A new pedestrian walkway built atop the old O&W Bridge provides the once missing link between these two halves of the old 36-mile rail line.

Some people would like to see a scenic railroad established along this old railbed; the train, they say, could also be used to haul freight at night. Conservationists favor using the railbed for a hiking trail or bicycle path; they oppose any more transportation into the gorge, which is designated wilderness. There are already plenty of roads into the gorge, they reason, and already a scenic railroad in the Kentucky portion of the park. Since little money is available for either option, the debate is academic for the time being.

From the bridge at the end of the trail, enjoy the view of rock bluffs overhead; below, you'll see rapids stretching upstream before fading around the bend. Retrace your walk to the Leatherwood Ford Area.

7 East Rim and Sunset Overlooks

0.1-mile loop and 1.3 miles one way
Easy
Level
Cautions: High cliffs
Connections: Leatherwood Ford Loop

Attractions: These overlooks provide panoramic views of the river gorge and Leatherwood Ford.

Trailhead: East from Leatherwood Ford 1.6 miles on TN297, or west on TN297 0.6 mile from the east entrance sign, turn west on the gravel road. Continue 0.7 mile to the turnaround at the end of the road.

Description: Walk the 0.1-mile loop from the turnaround to the East Rim Overlook. The right portion is suitable handicap access. A large wooden platform lets you poise at the edge of the canyon for a view of the Big South Fork River. To the left, you'll see a rock bluff that is the Sunset Overlook.

To get to that overlook, return to the parking area and go back along the road 0.4 mile to the sign for the East Rim Trailhead and the beginning of the Leatherwood Ford Loop on the north side of the road. On the south side of the road you'll see the beginning of the trail to Sunset Overlook.

After 0.1 mile, you'll pass by a small building and shooting range no longer available for public use. Enter the woods, pass by a pond, and you'll be on an old nature trail marked by interpretive numbers. This trail is a leftover from when the visitor center was located in what is now a maintenance area on TN297. The trail crosses a stream and skirts the back of the maintenance area, passes another pond, and joins a trail that leads 1.0 mile to the Sunset Overlook. From the overlook, you can see where North White Oak Creek joins the Big South Fork on the other side of the river.

East Rim Overlook

8 Leatherwood Ford Loop

3.2 miles
Difficult
Elevation change: 500 ft.
Cautions: High cliffs, stream crossings
Connections: John Muir Trail

Attractions: The upper part of the loop offers scenic views and is lined with blooming laurel in mid-May; in early spring, you'll walk through masses of wildflowers on the lower elevations as you approach the river.

Trailhead: East from Leatherwood Ford 1.6 miles on TN297, or west on TN297 0.6 mile from the park's east entrance sign, turn west on the gravel road just north of the park maintenance area. In 0.3 mile, a sign on the right signals the East Rim Trailhead and the Leatherwood Loop. Park here to hike the loop.

Description: From the sign, walk to the left, paralleling the road until you enter the woods and the trail becomes more obvious.

In 0.2 mile you will hit the Leatherwood Ford Loop. Turn left for the best approach. You'll cross a creek, join an old logging road for a short distance, and then drop among the rocks to a side trail at 0.4 mile that leads 0.1 mile to an overlook of the river with the bridge at Leatherwood Ford clearly visible.

From this side trail you will descend more obviously through switchbacks, crossing small streams that are easily forded, and past rock overhangs until the loop trail reaches the river at 1.4 miles. This section of the trail wanders through a garden of wildflowers in spring—foamflower, penstemon, geranium, columbine, solomon seal, phlox, cinquefoil, asters, crested dwarf iris, blood root, fire pink, may apple, dwarf dandelion, and more.

At the river the trail has joined the John Muir Trail. You can turn left here to reach the old O&W Railroad Bridge in 1.8 miles.

To continue the loop, turn right on the John Muir Trail, which is blazed with a blue silhouette of John Muir, and parallel the river. The trail eventually becomes a gravel path leading to Leatherwood Ford at 1.9 miles.

Right next to the Leatherwood Ford Bridge, turn right and go up the rock steps beside the bridge. After topping out on the road, walk up the road, crossing over a side creek, until you get to a Leatherwood Loop sign with its back to you. Turn right into the woods to complete the loop back to the top of the canyon rim.

This part of the loop follows along the creek that you crossed on the road as it cascades among boulders on its way down the mountain, creating many picturesque spots with small waterfalls and slots of rushing water in coves of rhododendron and hemlock. Sections follow the old wagon road that once led to Leatherwood Ford. Once you reach the canyon top, you'll follow the border between field and forest until you cross a footbridge near a pond. A short hike returns you to the beginning of the loop trail and then back to the trailhead.

The last time we hiked this second half of the trail, a virtual road had been cut through the area. A year before when we hiked the trail the Army Corps of Engineers had contractors in here to lay a waterline to the restrooms at the parking area at Leatherwood Ford. The trail was nearly obliterated in a muddy swath that was cut down the slope, presumably to give access for the heavy machinery that did the digging. Although the Corps has enthusiastically taken on its new role as preservationist, the development at times gets out of hand, as it has here. The contractors have made an attempt to repair the damage with small diversion dams of stone and logs and have thrown branches on the naked ground, all to prevent erosion. But the scar that is left will take many years to heal. Hopefully when you hike the trail, the area will be rehabilitated enough you can enjoy what is left of the wilderness character.

⑨ Dome Rockhouse Trail

1.5 miles one way
Moderate
Elevation loss: 100 ft.
Cautions: Creek crossings, ridge ascents
Connections: Big Island

Attractions: The rockhouse featuring a dome-shaped room along this trail is a unique geologic structure.

Trailhead: From the junction of Bandy Creek Road and TN297, turn east on TN297 for 7.1 miles, crossing Leatherwood Ford along the way. Or from Oneida, drive west on TN297 4.8 miles, to Station Camp Road. A sign directs you northeast toward Station Camp. After 1.9 miles the road becomes a dirt road. Watch for a BSFNRRA sign at 3.9 miles and soon after you'll see the Station Camp East Trailhead sign on the right. You can reach the Dome Rockhouse from this trailhead in 2.2 miles. For a shorter hike, continue along the road until at 6.4 miles you see a sign on the right directing you to the Station Camp East Trailhead. From here the Dome Rockhouse is 1.3 miles.

Description: For the shorter hike, follow the trail toward the Station Camp East Trailhead. From the road you'll quickly drop into a hemlock forest on a trail blazed with a horse head image; this is one of the park's horse trails.

As you cross a wooden bridge and drop to a forest floor carpeted with fern, you'll pass dripping rock bluffs to your right and straight ahead. Small streams of water spilling over smooth rock lips form a pool at the base of the bluffs. The trail then ascends to a switchback right that signals a climb above the bluff where the trail levels off on top of the ridge.

Cross a roadbed at 0.7 mile and descend gradually. The trail crosses a jeep road at 0.9 mile and continues to descend through the woods, joining a spring on the left of the trail. At 1.3 miles a sign points right for the 0.2-mile hike down past horse rails to the rockhouse. The cave entryway opens to a recessed room where, once your eyes adjust to the dark, you'll see the large hemispherical ceiling.

From the side trail to the Dome Rockhouse, you can continue along the main trail to get to the Station Camp East Trailhead in 2.0 miles. About half a mile along this section of the trail you'll find the junction for the trail that heads north to Big Island, an island in the middle of the Big South Fork River. Because of the shallow ford at Big Island, an Indian trail and later a wagon road crossed the river at that point on the way to Monticello, Kentucky. If you ford the river, you can link up with the John Muir Trail.

From the Dome Rockhouse, retrace your steps back to your parking place; you can then continue another 0.6 mile down the dirt road to have a look at Chimney Rocks, the most obvious rocks just off the road to the left. Hard sandstone caps protecting softer layers below are responsible for the formation of these tall rock pillars.

The continuation of the road from the Chimney Rocks down to Station Camp is passable but very rough. The park staff plans to improve the road sometime in the future. Check to see if the work has been done before you attempt the road in a passenger car.

The Station Camp area, primarily on the west side of the river, was first the gathering place for early long hunters. They and their descendents settled the valley along Station Camp Creek so that by 1850 there were over 100 people living on subsistence farms in the valley. Nothing of the community remains except a small cemetery or two and Jonathan Blevins' house at Charit Creek Lodge about 4 miles up Station Camp Creek.

At Station Camp, there is a ford across the river that is part of the horse trail system. It is possible to link up with the John Muir Trail on the west side of the river near where Station Camp Creek flows into the Big South Fork. To the south, the John Muir Trail leads to the Grand Gap Loop. To the north, the JMT eventually crosses Parch Corn Creek near the John Litton Cabin, built in 1881 by Litton before he moved south and built the farmstead on the John Litton Farm Loop trail. Beyond the cabin, the JMT then veers to the northwest just before Big Island.

Chimney Rocks

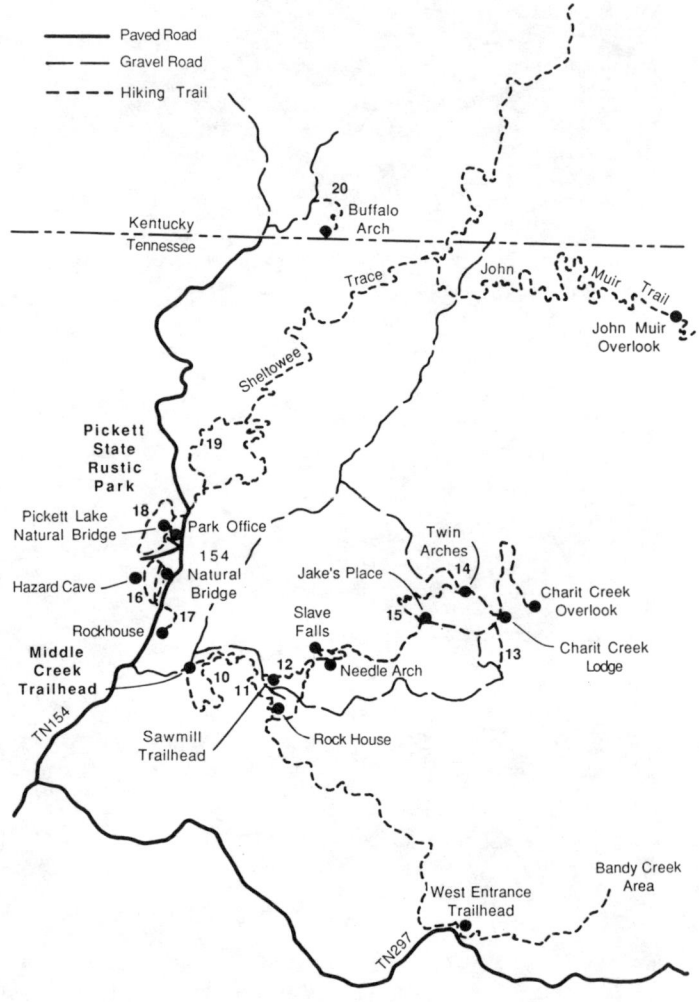

Middle Creek and Pickett State Park

10 Middle Creek Nature Trail

3.5-mile loop
Moderate
Elevation change: 100 ft.
Cautions: Occasional stream crossings, boulder passages,
mud holes on jeep trail section
Connections: Indian Rock House, Bandy Creek

Attractions: This loop takes you by an impressive array of cliff walls and rock overhangs.

Trailhead: North on TN154 1.9 miles from the junction of 154 and 297 west of Bandy Creek and north of Jamestown, or south on TN154 0.8 miles from the Pickett State Park entrance, turn east on a dirt road. A sign says "Twin Arches." The Middle Creek Trailhead and parking area is on the right in 0.7 miles.

Description: From the trailhead sign, walk into the forest along a gravel road about 50 yards to a sign indicating the Middle Creek Nature Trail both straight ahead and to the left. Other trails can also be reached to the left.

To do the nature trail clockwise, turn left into the woods on a footpath. Along this section, the trail parallels the dirt road coming in from the highway, so you'll catch glimpses of it on the left through the trees. You'll encounter many white-tailed deer that bound away as you approach, if no one has preceded you and already scared them away. The Shawnees called the Cumberland Plateau, "Ouasioto," meaning "mountains where the deer are plentiful." The end of May, you'll also find the blooming laurel plentiful.

At about 0.7 mile, the trail descends gradually and then more steeply with a few switchbacks. At one mile, you'll reach a left turnoff for Indian Rock House at a distance of 1.5 miles. You can also take this left turn to the Bandy Creek Campground in 10.9 miles or you can link up with the Slave Falls and Twin Arches/ Charit Creek Loop trails.

To continue the loop, bear right. Cross a creek on planks and climb until you encounter a rock bluff on the right with the creek running along the base of the rock wall. Soon you'll reach the first of the rock overhangs. From here until you climb back to the top of the bluff a mile and a half later, you'll pass eight rock overhangs forming hollows in the rock walls, some quite large. Most of these have a trickle of water running from underneath, an erosion process that helped create the recesses. You'll easily cross these creeks on stepping stones. Occasionally, the trail meanders under the overhangs along their sandy floors and through boulders piled in front of the openings. A recent rain will leave small waterfalls that drop off the lips of rock overhead.

At around 2.0 miles you'll climb up a small ridge and walk along the ridge before dropping below the bluff line once again. You'll pass more of the rock overhangs.

At about 2.5 miles, the trail passes along a sweeping rock wall, until the path drops and crosses a creek on a boardwalk and then crosses again a little later. Keep straight ahead when the trail crosses an old logging road. At about 3.0 miles, you come to the last of the rock overhangs, cross a creek, climb some rock steps, and walk along the base of the rock wall. The trail turns and climbs to the top of the ridge. Swing right and follow the trail along the ridgeline. When the trail links up with a jeep road, turn right along the road to complete the loop in 3.5 miles while skirting several large mudholes.

11 Indian Rock House Trail

2.5 miles one way
Easy
Elevation loss: 100 ft.
Cautions: None
Connections: Middle Creek Nature Trail,
Bandy Creek, Slave Falls

Attractions: A deep rockhouse stands along the way as you descend toward Laurel Fork Creek.

Trailhead: Follow the directions to the Middle Creek Trailhead described in Trail #10.

Description: From the Middle Creek Trailhead, you can reach several trails, including the trail to Indian Rock House. Walk the Middle Creek Nature Trail clockwise until in one mile you reach the junction of the Indian Rock House Trail. Turn left onto the trail. From this junction the Indian Rock House is 1.5 miles.

Walking through a forest of hardwood and pine for 0.8 mile, you'll first reach the junction for Slave Falls and the Sawmill Trailhead. To walk these trails, you would turn left and cross the dirt road coming in from the highway. On the other side of the road, Slave Falls is 1.1 miles straight ahead and the Sawmill Trailhead is to the right 0.1 mile. The trailhead can also be reached along the road, and you can begin your walk to Indian Rock House from this trailhead if you want a shorter walk.

From this Slave Falls junction, Indian Rock House is just 0.7 mile. Along the way, you'll pass two open areas where either fire and/or wind thinned the trees and the forest has yet to fully recover. Then the trail drops among rock bluffs and crosses a creek on a boardwalk. Ferns, cinquefoil, bluets, and ground pine line the trail. At 0.6 mile, the trail gently drops to where an old logging road comes in from the left. From here it's just 0.1 mile to the rockhouse. Continue dropping, cross a creek, and walk up to Indian Rock House, a huge hole in the rock bluff.

Such rock recesses are commonly called "rockhouses" because the prehistoric Indians that once inhabited the region lived in them at times. Few of the historic Indians, the Cherokees and Shawnees, lived year-round on the plateau, but until the whitemen took their land, both groups claimed the wilderness that separated their settlements as their hunting ground. The Cherokees came from their towns in what is now eastern Tennessee, North Carolina, and Georgia, while the Shawnees came from their settlements along the Ohio River. On their hunting expeditions for the deer, buffalo, and elk that once grazed the Cumberland Plateau, the Indians camped under the rock overhangs for the shelter they provided, as did the explorers, long hunters, and settlers that came after them.

From Indian Rock House, retrace your steps back to the Middle Creek Trailhead. But if you want to walk farther, you can continue on the trail past Indian Rock House and climb to a trail junction in 0.3 mile. From the junction, Slave Falls can be reached in a little more than a mile to the left after crossing the dirt road that comes in from the highway. To the right is the long trail that crosses Laurel Fork Creek in about 0.6 mile and passes the West Entrance Trailhead on TN 297 in 6.0 miles (on some park maps called the "Bandy Creek Ranger Station Trailhead" because a ranger station was once planned there, but no longer). From the West Entrance Trailhead, the trail continues on to the Bandy Creek Campground near the visitor center in a total distance of 9.3 miles from Indian Rock House.

12 Slave Falls Loop

3.2 miles
Moderate
Elevation change: 100 ft.
Cautions: Boulder passages
Connections: Jake's Place, Indian Rock House,
Bandy Creek

Attractions: Along this loop you'll find 60-foot Slave Falls and, a little beyond the loop, Needle Arch.

Trailhead: Follow the directions in Trail #10 to the Middle Creek Trailhead and continue another 0.2 mile to where the road forks, with Twin Arches to the left, Slave Falls and Charit Creek Lodge to the right. Turn right 1.1 miles to the Sawmill Trailhead.

Description: From the Sawmill Trailhead, walk left 0.1 mile to the Slave Falls Loop. From here Slave Falls is 1.1 miles to the right. If you were to turn left on the loop, you'd cross the road and connect with the Indian Rock House Trail.

Turn right to walk the loop clockwise. You'll pass through a mixed pine-hemlock-hardwood forest until you cross a fern-shrouded creek on a plank walkway. Around 0.8 mile, you'll get your first glimpse of the hollow that contains the waterfall.

A sign at 1.0 mile directs you to turn right to continue on the Slave Falls Loop, but first go straight ahead a short distance to a left turn that takes you 0.2 mile to the waterfall overlook. The trail drops among thick understory over rock steps and passes beside a rock wall through boulders. At the end you'll find a slender waterfall splashing in a pit among the rocks below with a large amphitheater behind.

The hard sandstone that caps the Cumberland Plateau permits such dramatic formations. When a creek finds a break in the sandstone, it quickly washes away the softer layers of rock below, creating a waterfall. The water then continues to erode rock underlying the lip of sandstone that clings to the top of the waterfall, creating a natural amphitheater.

This side trail ends at the falls. You can get to the other side of the waterfall by returning to the main trail and continuing on for a half mile to another side trail to the left that takes you 0.2 mile to an overlook on the other side of the falls. You could then continue on the main trail 1.5 miles all the way to Jake's Place, which is on the Twin Arches/Charit Creek Loop.

If you decide not to walk the extra distance to the far side of Slave Falls, at least continue on the trail a quarter mile to Needle Arch. A sign directs you right on a path to the top of the delicate natural arch. Again, it's the sandstone that makes the geologic formation possible—only when the rock is very hard can such a thin ribbon of rock remain suspended.

From Needle Arch, retrace your steps past Slave Falls to return to the Slave Falls Loop. To complete the loop, turn uphill. You'll follow an old jeep road until the trail hits a dirt road. Turn left on the road, which then runs into another dirt road, which is the road in from the highway. Immediately across the road, the trail reenters the woods and intertwines with old jeep trails until at 1.2 miles from Slave Falls you reach a junction. To the left, you can walk 9 miles to the Bandy Creek Campground. Turn right, you'll find the Indian Rock House in 0.3 mile.

After passing the rockhouse, follow the Indian Rock House Trail 0.7 mile to the junction sign that directs you right to the Sawmill Trailhead. Once you cross the road, you will have completed the Slave Falls Loop.

13 Charit Creek Lodge Trail

0.8 mile one way
Moderate
Elevation loss: 500 ft.
Cautions: Stairs, creek crossing, steep return ascent
Connections: Twin Arches/Charit Creek Loop

Attractions: The trail leads to an old homesite/hunting lodge that is now Charit Creek Lodge.

Trailhead: Follow the directions in Trail #12 to the Sawmill Trailhead. Here the road forks again. The right fork leads 0.3 mile to the site of an old fire tower where only a cabin and the tower's foundations remain. Take the left fork 3.0 miles to parking for the Lodge trailhead. The dirt road actually continues all the way to the Lodge, but it is blocked to vehicles just beyond the parking area. The last time we drove this road to the trailhead, it was in very bad shape, although work on the road was scheduled in the coming months. If the road has not been improved by the time you get there, you may want to walk to the Lodge using Trails #14 and #15 for a 1.8-mile walk.

Description: From the parking area, you could walk 1.5 miles along the blocked road to the Lodge, but for a shorter and more pleasant walk take the trail at the end of the parking area.

You'll descend through switchbacks and a few steps about 0.2 mile to the top of wooden stairs that take you down a rock bluff; a creek pouroff is on the left. The trail bears right down stone steps, following the rock bluff. The trail then turns away from the bluff and descends by switchbacks through a dense forest of hardwoods and hemlocks with the creek spilling down on your left. You'll pass large beech trees and ferns littering the ground. In spring you'll find numerous wildflowers. As the trail descends through large boulders, watch for stone crop, trillium, and rue anemone growing on the rock. Along the way you'll also see hepatica, chickweed, phlox, violets, cinquefoil, and more.

Charit Creek Lodge

When you bottom out at 0.7 mile, you'll be walking along Station Camp Creek on the left that flows east to the Big South Fork River. To get to the Lodge, you must ford this creek. Follow the trail to the creek's edge, and you'll find stepping stones to help you across. Just before the creek crossing, you'll see where Charit Creek joins Station Camp Creek on the other side.

Charit Creek Lodge consists of several structures: a large central building with outlying cabins and even a solar bathhouse. The Lodge is a concession operated by LeConte Lodge, Ltd., the same group that operates the LeConte Lodge in the Great Smoky Mountains National Park. You can get meals with your lodging; reservations are needed. This is a favorite place for horse riders who can leave their horses in the large barn set apart from the central complex.

Charit Creek was originally the homeplace of Jonathan Blevins, a long hunter who first came into the area in the late 1700s. Around 1817, he built the two-room cabin with a central chimney that is still there. Blevins died in 1863 from bee stings and is buried in the Blevins Cemetery about two miles below the Lodge on Station Camp Creek.

Later, others lived here—Jonathan Burke, William Riley Hatfield (both of whom lie in a small cemetery near the Lodge), and Oscar Blevins with his father John (who were descendants of Jonathan Blevins and who built the present barn). The last family to live here, the Phillips, sold the homesite to Joe Simpson around 1963, who operated it as the Parch Corn Hunting Lodge until 1982, when the Corps purchased it for the park. The Lodge was renamed Charit Creek, after the creek that flows beside the Lodge into Station Camp Creek that passes in front.

If you walk to the left after entering the Lodge area, you'll find a bridge across Charit Creek that connects with the Twin Arches/Charit Creek Loop Trail. Just before the bridge, you'll also find the junction for horse trails. Long Trail to the right will take you to the Big South Fork in 4.1 miles. This is also part of the 9.9-mile Hatfield Ridge Loop. If you were to walk straight ahead on the loop, following Charit Creek upstream, you would reach in about 3 miles the Charit Creek Overlook, which can be seen high on the bluff above the Lodge. This is not an easy walk though because the horses have made a mess of the trail.

14 Twin Arches Trail

0.7 mile one way
Easy
Elevation loss: 100 ft.
Cautions: Steep stairways
Connections: Twin Arches/Charit Creek Loop

Attractions: The Twin Arches are two of the largest arches in the eastern United States aligned nearly end to end.

Trailhead: Follow the directions in Trail #10 to the Middle Creek Trailhead and continue another 0.2 mile to where the road forks, with Twin Arches to the left, Slave Falls and Charit Creek Lodge to the right. Turn left. In 3.0 miles you'll reach the turnoff to the right for Twin Arches. It's another 2.0 miles to the trailhead.

Description: From the trailhead, you'll enter the woods and descend steps through a mixed pine and hardwood forest to a junction at 0.2 mile. A sign directs you to turn left to Twin Arches, but you can do a loop by continuing straight ahead.

The trail becomes a wood-bordered walkway that leads up a knoll. You'll climb some stairs to get to the top for your first views of the surrounding canyons—Station Camp Creek to the west and Charit Creek to the east and in the distance the Big South Fork. Continue across the knoll, and you'll descend by a long stairway. The trail then leads out onto the back of the North Arch, although from your perspective you'll appear to be standing on a ridge. You'll see bare rock and patches of reindeer moss.

A wooden walkway leads to another elaborate flight of stairs that takes you down to the base of the arches. Before descending, you can continue along the ridgeline onto the back of the South Arch. With some difficulty, you can climb to a peak atop the South Arch from which you have wide views of the landscape, a sea of color in fall. Once you have descended to the base of the arches, you'll see you have been walking across the twin bridges.

South Arch

Twin Arches is the most spectacular geologic formation in the Big South Fork area. The park has many arches, but nowhere else do you find two large arches so close together. The complex is so large there is virtually no place from which to see the entire structure at once. The South Arch, the largest on the Cumberland Plateau, has a span of 135 feet and a clearance of 70 feet. The North Arch has a span of 93 feet and a clearance of 51 feet.

The arches were formed by headward erosion, a process in which a gully slowly advances up a hill, perhaps a gully on each side. Eventually the eroding gullies open a hole through the ridge that broadens through continued erosion and weathering until the hole is quite large, as at Twin Arches.

The Twin Arches complex also includes two tunnels. At the south end of South Arch, you'll find the West Tunnel, so named because it is on the west side. The tunnel is 88 feet long and was caused by widening of a joint. A much smaller passage, East Tunnel, can be found on the east side between the two arches; in fact, under the stairway about halfway down. Water moving through rock created the East Tunnel. So within this one complex, arches were formed by three different processes.

Under the North Arch, you'll be standing on the Twin Arches/Charit Creek Loop, which you can hike by following the trail to the west toward Jake's Place. Bear to the east to complete the short loop back to the Twin Arches Trailhead. You will ascend two sets of stairs before rejoining the main trail.

The trail back passes over several small creeks on planks. The water flows from the base of the ridge—active headward erosion that may in time add other arches to the Twin Arches complex.

15 Twin Arches/Charit Creek Loop

4.6 miles
Moderate
Elevation change: 400 ft.
Cautions: Steps, boulder passages, stream crossings
Connections: Twin Arches, Charit Creek, Slave Falls

Attractions: The trail loops by Twin Arches, rockhouses, Jake's Place, and Charit Creek Lodge.

Trailhead: Three trails give access to the Twin Arches/Charit Creek Loop: the Twin Arches Trail, the Charit Creek Lodge Trail, and the Slave Falls Loop. Follow the directions to the trailhead of any of these three and walk the trail to reach the loop. The shortest route is to walk in on the 0.7-mile Twin Arches Trail.

Description: At the base of the Twin Arches, you'll find a sign that points east to Charit Creek Lodge in 1.1 miles. But to walk the loop counterclockwise, pass under the North Arch where a sign directs you toward the northwest 2.0 miles to Jake's Place.

The trail skirts the ridge, passing by several rockhouses where in wet weather water trickles over the edge of the rock above to plink on your head as you pass. Flowers are frequent in spring; you'll find laurel, iris, and columbine. At about one mile, watch for an overhang where erosion has bored a hole through the rock, creating a tunnel to the ridgetop. This is an arch in formation; erosion will continue to separate the outer strip of rock from the wall.

The trail loops south, leaving the ridge. In July, watch for blueberries. You'll begin dropping into the valley created by Station Camp Creek. At the lower elevations the trail passes by more wildflowers: fire pink, fleabane daisy, dwarf dandelion, cinquefoil.

When you reach creek level, you'll pass through cedar bottoms, crossing a side stream on a boardwalk and stepping stones. At 2.0 miles, the trail enters a meadow known as "Jake's Place." Here, you'll find the junction of the trail to Slave Falls, which is at a distance of 1.5 miles.

The homesite here probably dates to about the same time as the old Jonathan Blevins home that became Charit Creek Lodge. Several families lived at Jake's Place; Jacob Blevins, Jr., and his wife, Viannah, were the last. A grandson of Jonathan Blevins, Jacob, Jr., was known as "Jakey" and in later years as "Uncle Jake." Jakey died in 1935, followed a decade later by Vi; they both lie in the Katie Blevins Cemetery near the Clara Sue Blevins Historic Site at Bandy Creek. Jakey's father, Jacob Blevins, was the first to be buried in the cemetery along with his wife Catherine, who was known as "Katie."

Jake's Place is marked by a solitary stone chimney. Joe Simpson bought the home and had it torn down and moved to Charit Creek, which at the time was his hunting lodge. The two small bunk cabins at the Lodge are made of Uncle Jake's logs.

From Jake's Place, cross a side stream on a plank bridge, and follow the trail that parallels Station Camp Creek on the right. You'll find nice wading pools in the creek. At 1.2 miles from Jake's Place, the trail joins a gravel road, which is the continuation of the road down from the parking area to the Charit Creek Lodge. Walk the road to the Lodge. If you want to enter the Lodge, you must cross Charit Creek on a bridge.

From the Lodge, it is 1.1 miles back to Twin Arches. The trail first parallels Charit Creek through a mixed hardwood forest. This is a good section for wildflowers in spring; you'll see bluets, cinquefoil, crested dwarf iris, violets of several kinds, chickweed, rue anemone, dogwood, and more. The trail then climbs steeply with many log steps and switchbacks until you arrive at the base of the arches. You must then return along the Twin Arches Trail to the parking area for a total distance of 6.0 miles.

Jake's Place

16 Hazard Cave Loop

2.5 miles
Easy
Elevation change: 100 ft.
Cautions: Steep concrete stairs
Connections: Natural Bridge, Indian Rockhouse

Attractions: Near the Middle Creek area, adjacent to the BSFNRRA, lies Tennessee's Pickett State Rustic Park, known for its arches and rockhouses. Among these you'll find Hazard Cave and, above the cave's opening, Hazard Cave Window.

Trailhead: North 0.8 mile from the Middle Creek Trailhead turnoff on TN154, you'll enter the state park. Continue north 0.2 mile to a turnout on the left, which is the trailhead for Hazard Cave.

Description: From the parking area, Hazard Cave is a quarter-mile hike. To get to the Hazard Cave Loop, follow the trail into the woods.

You'll drop along slag-filled steps to some concrete steps. At the bottom, you are on the 2.5-mile Hazard Cave Loop Trail. Turn left to first go by Hazard Cave. You'll descend another long flight of concrete stairs and drop to a boardwalk at the base of a long rock wall that contains Hazard Cave, a large cave with a sand floor.

If you walk all the way to the back of the cave and turn back toward the entrance, you'll see a slit of light at the top of the cave opening. This is Hazard Cave Window, a small arch caused by sagging of the rock layers at the mouth of the cave.

You can retrace your steps from the cave for a round-trip hike of half a mile. Across the road from the parking area, you'll find the Indian Rockhouse Trail.

Or you can continue on from Hazard Cave to complete the loop, which eventually joins up with trails to the Natural Bridge. This arch is sometimes called "Highway 154 Natural Bridge" because it is right beside the road. You can simply drive the highway from the Hazard Cave turnout another 0.2 mile into the state park to reach the parking area for the Natural Bridge. From the road you must climb down steps to get to the arch, which with a span of 86 feet and a clearance of 23 feet, was likely formed by the widening of a joint between the arch and the ridge behind. This is an exceptionally thin arch of hard sandstone.

17 Indian Rockhouse Trail

0.2 mile one way
Easy
Elevation Loss: 100 ft.
Cautions: None
Connections: Hazard Cave Trail

Attractions: The trail ends at a sweeping rock overhang that may be largest in the Big South Fork region.

Trailhead: Follow the directions in Trail #16 to the Hazard Cave Trail parking area. The Indian Rockhouse Trail begins across the road.

Description: Not to be confused with the Indian Rock House Trail in the Middle Creek area, this Indian Rockhouse Trail drops gradually 0.1 mile among laurel and mixed hardwoods to an overlook on the right and the sound of dripping water. You'll see the rockhouse below and to the right. But you cannot get the full feel of the place without entering the rockhouse.

So continue from here as the trail drops and then circles right to the rockhouse. Although the trail ends, you can enjoy a walk through the massive 250-degree circular structure. A small pool at the center is fed by water falling about 60 feet from the rim above.

18 Lake Trail Loop

2.5 miles
Easy
Elevation change: 100 ft.
Cautions: Swinging bridge
Connections: Lake View Trail, Bluff Trail,
Ladder Trail, Island Trail

Attractions: This trail loops around the lake that is the center of Pickett State Rustic Park and passes by an arch that spans part of the lake.

Trailhead: Entering Pickett State Park from the south on TN154, turn left into the picnic area just before the state park office. Begin your walk at the swinging bridge that crosses Pickett Lake from the parking area.

Description: After crossing the swinging bridge, turn right; to the left is the Lake View Trail that follows Pickett Lake to the south for three-quarters of a mile. To the north, the Lake Trail climbs some rock stairs and then follows the bluff beside the lake with views of the swimming and boating area. There are several side trails, but just stay with the red blaze to keep to the main trail.

At 0.2 mile, the trail then switches back left and soon forks; keep straight ahead following the red blaze. After about 0.7 mile, you'll find a rest shelter to the right where you can sit and look out over the lake.

At one mile a short side trail leads down to the Thompson Creek Dam built by the Civilian Conservation Corps in the 1930s at the same time they built the old cabins and the swimming pavilion in the park. From the top of the dam, you'll get your first view of Pickett Lake Natural Bridge stretching across an arm of the lake created by the dam. Because of the natural bridge, the lake is sometimes called "Arch Lake." It's possible to walk out a few steps on top of the dam, but use caution so that you don't fall; you'll have a good view of the lake spilling over the dam into Thompson Creek below with the natural bridge in front of you.

The bridge is an incised meander. At some time in the past, Thompson Creek folded back on itself to create a meander and eventually punched a hole through the ridge to make the bridge. The bridge was eventually left high and dry as the creek continued to erode, cutting its valley deeper. At one time a narrow-gauge railway used to haul lumber out of the area paralleled Thompson Creek and passed under the natural bridge. The construction of the Thompson Creek Dam brought the water back to a level with the bridge opening. Today you can rent boats at the state park and float under the bridge.

Continue on the Lake Trail with a slight climb, then level off to a gradual downhill. At about 1.5 miles you'll come to the junction with the one-mile Bluff Trail to the left that leads to TN154. Bear right, passing down through rhododendron to a footbridge over Thompson Creek below the dam. Here's a great place to pull off your shoes and go wading.

A slight climb from the creek takes you through hemlock and rhododendron to a junction with the one-mile Ladder Trail, a portion of which connects with the park campground. You'll also pass a branch in the Lake Trail that has a red blaze like the main trail; this is a side trail to another rest shelter that eventually rejoins the main trail.

At 2.0 miles, you'll reach the junction with the half-mile Island Trail that passes over the top of Pickett Lake Natural Bridge; to the right you can see the Thompson Creek Dam. The Island Trail then loops around the peninsula past another rest shelter and returns to the natural bridge and rejoins the Lake Trail. Continuing on the Lake Trail, you'll pass behind the park chalets and then wander through the boating and swimming area. Just before arriving back at the picnic area, the trail crosses a footbridge.

19 Hidden Passage Trail

10-mile loop
Easy
Level
Cautions: High bluffs, stream crossings
Connections: Rock Creek Trail, Sheltowee Trace,
John Muir Trail

Attractions: Small arches, waterfalls, numerous rockhouses, and the Hidden Passage make this the most interesting trail in Pickett State Park. You can camp anywhere away from the trail.

Trailhead: Head north from the park office on TN154. In 0.3 mile you'll see the Hidden Passage Trailhead on the right. There's room for only two vehicles to park.

Description: As you walk into the woods to begin the Hidden Passage Trail, you'll find the way marked with green blazes and occasionally the shape of a white turtle. The turtle signifies this is also part of the Sheltowee Trace National Recreation Trail, which has traveled south from Kentucky through the northwest portion of the BSFNRRA to end at Pickett State Park. Although we saw no blazes of John Muir, this part of the Hidden Passage Trail is also one alternative for the ending of the John Muir Trail, which has traveled north from Leatherwood Ford in the BSFNRRA and then swung west to also end at Pickett State Park. The other ending for the John Muir Trail branches off before it reaches the Hidden Passage Trail and enters the northern end of Pickett.

The trail passes through woods of pine, mixed hardwood, and laurel. In spring you'll notice birdfoot violets, yellow stargrass, and bluets. Soon after beginning the trail, climbing fern decorate the shrubs on your left. Thompson Creek flows downstream on your right, creating a gorge that will grow deeper as you continue on the trail.

You'll follow a side creek upstream and cross at a spillway. The hollow of the stream contains hemlock and rhododendron.

This stretch of trail is typical of the Hidden Passage Trail, meandering across the top of the plateau in predominantly pine and mixed hardwoods and periodically dropping into coves where the hemlock and rhododendron predominate.

At 0.5 mile, you'll reach the junction with the loop part of the trail, you can walk either left or right, but the best approach is to walk right, hiking counterclockwise. You'll soon encounter a small arch created by a short column of rock supporting an overhang. You'll turn right and descend to a large overhang that serves as a passageway for the trail. This is the Hidden Passage.

At about 0.7 mile, a short side trail takes you down to the foot of Crystal Falls. This tributary spills down two steps into a green pool of water before making its way to Thompson Creek.

Back on the main trail, you'll climb up stone steps and then cross the stream above Crystal Falls. You'll have to hop across; since you are at the top of the falls, watch your step. The trail parallels the gorge for a time and then turns away from the gorge, passing through reindeer moss and blueberries that are ripe in July. You'll find the loop periodically swerves from the edge of the gorge but then later returns.

At about 1.3 miles, the trail reaches a bare rock overlook of the gorge and then turns away from the gorge edge. You'll cross a jeep road at 1.5 miles. Then at 1.8 miles the trail swings sharp right while a side trail to the left leads to a low rockhouse. From here the trail passes many rockhouses and overhangs some quite large and long. Many of these have benches inside, built by the Civilian Conservation Corps in the 1930s when the park was being developed out of Stearns Coal and Lumber Company land.

At 2.1 miles you'll dip into a long rockhouse sheltered by thick rhododendron and with a wet-weather waterfall in the center. When you emerge from the rockhouse, watch for a huge hemlock balanced at an angle on your left. At 2.4 miles the trail passes under a powerline.

At 2.8 miles you'll reach a narrow section of the trail with a rock bluff on your left and a dropoff into Thompson Creek Gorge on your right. Around a point, you'll find a long rock overhang and then a long rock wall. At 3.2 miles, the trail crosses a stream on a stone walkway. Then at 4.0 miles you'll come to a large rockhouse that sweeps around in a 180-degree curve; a small waterfall spills from the lip of rock overhead. Then another rock overhang, and at 4.2 miles you'll reach the 1-mile side trail to Double Falls, which is on a tributary of Thompson Creek. The side trail, marked with a white blaze, drops from the bluff to Thompson Creek, a good campsite. You must wade across to get to the waterfall.

From the side trail junction, you'll switchback up and walk along the bluff to Thompson Overlook at 4.4 miles, where you'll have views of the gorge. You'll find here the end of a jeep road that has come from the Group Camp in the park. You could shorten your walk by taking this road left.

At 5.0 miles, you'll cross a stream on a bridge and come to a junction with the Rock Creek Trail marked by a brown blaze. You'll also notice the white turtle blaze follows this trail. Both the Sheltowee Trace and the John Muir Trail leave the Hidden Passage Trail at this point, following the Rock Creek Trail.

After this junction, the trail switchbacks up, crosses a jeep road, and switchbacks down into a hollow and to a junction with the one-mile Tunnel Trail marked with a blue blaze at 5.4 miles. This side trail leads to an abandoned railroad tunnel and to a junction with the Rock Creek Trail that has made a 7-mile loop from the last junction. The tunnel is left over from the time when lumber and coal were hauled out of the Big South Fork area. The abandoned tunnel is dangerous and should not be entered; a faint trail up and over connects with the Rock Creek Trail.

From the Tunnel Trail junction, you'll switchback up and walk along the bluff of the canyon of Rock Creek. The trail bears away from the canyon, crosses a jeep road, and passes under a powerline at about 6.2 miles. At 7.5 miles, you'll emerge onto the road running from the Group Camp with Thompson Creek Overlook to the left. Turn right and walk down the dirt road to the Group Camp; bear left around the compound until at 8.5 miles the trail turns left off the road and once more enters the woods. You'll walk along the top of a circular rock wall and at the far end pass over a small arch.

The trail descends to a rockhouse and at 9.1 miles crosses a stream at the top of a small falls. The trail ascends and crosses an old road and drops to the junction at 9.5 miles where you first encountered the loop. It's then a half mile back to the trailhead.

Hidden Passage

20 Buffalo Arch Trail

0.8 mile one way
Moderate
Elevation loss: 100 ft.
Cautions: Large chunks of slag dumped in the jeep road
Connections: Parkers Mountain Trail

Attractions: At the end of this secluded trail, you'll find the unique Buffalo Arch.

Trailhead: From the Pickett State Park office, drive north on TN154 5.0 miles to the Kentucky State line. Here the paved highway becomes a gravel road. In another 0.3 mile, turn right on KY562 and enter the Daniel Boone National Forest, which abuts the BSFNRRA on the north. In another 0.7 mile, turn right on KY6305. Because of the roughness of the road from here on, we recommend not proceeding without a four-wheel drive, unless the Forest Service has improved the road by the time you get there. Park along the road in a convenient place, and on foot make a right turn down a steep dirt road.

Description: A short distance down the road, you'll reach the junction for the Parkers Mountain Trail, a Forest Service trail that heads north to the Great Meadows Campground. Continue straight ahead on the dirt road where in places slag has been dumped to fill mud holes. The walking is difficult because the slag pieces are so large.

The jeep road eventually forks; stay to the right. In about half a mile from where you started walking, you'll reach a turnaround in the road, although the road actually keeps going. The Buffalo Arch Trail heads into the woods on the right. The trail descends into a cove, crosses a creek over a metal culvert, and ends under the arch in about a quarter mile.

Buffalo Arch is little known because of the difficulty of finding it and the particularly secluded section of the national forest in which it stands. But the arch is well worth all the trouble to get to it. The huge arch is actually at the end of a ridge. The ridgeline descends across the back of the arch into the small valley created by the nearby creek. So the arch looks like a flying buttress holding up the hillside; one end attached to the ridge, the other resting on the ground.

Buffalo Arch

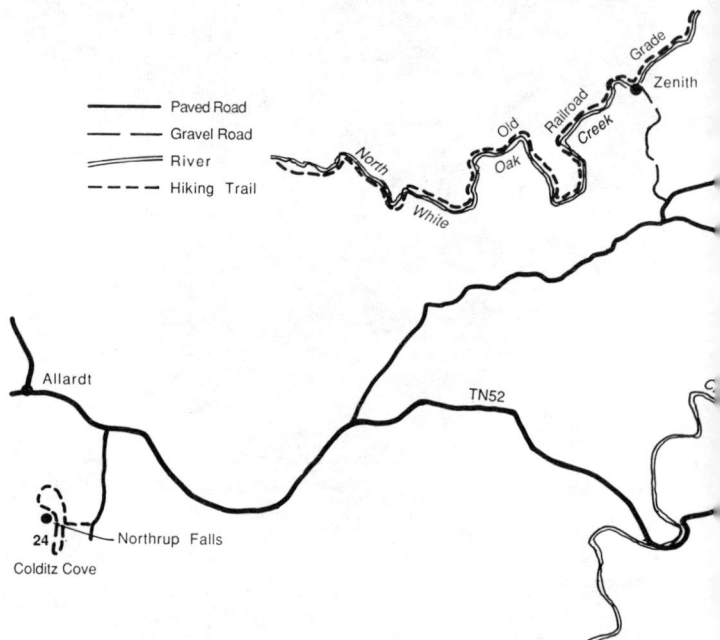

Burnt Mill and Rugby

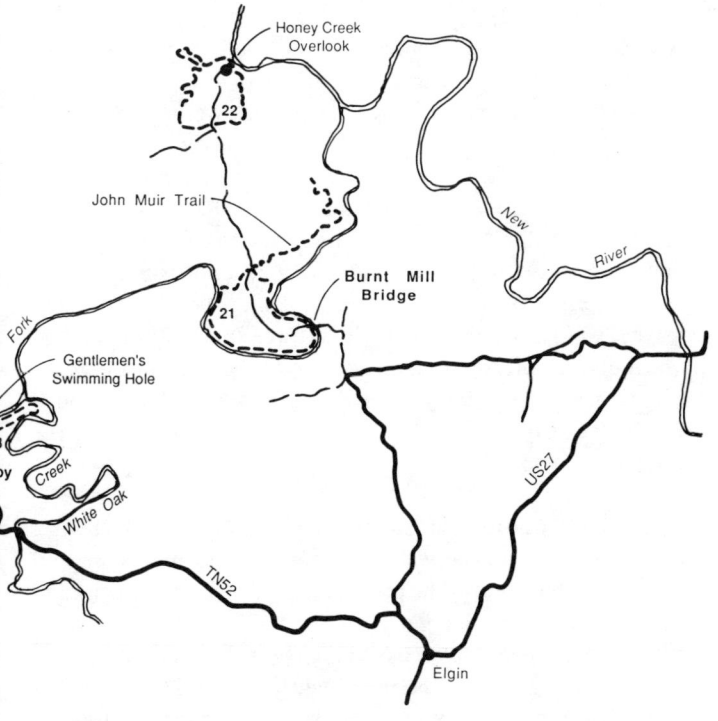

21 Burnt Mill Bridge Loop

4.3 miles
Moderate
Elevation change: 200 ft.
Cautions: Stairs
Connections: John Muir Trail

Attractions: For about 3 miles of its total length, this loop trail parallels the Clear Fork River with several places to get down to good wading pools; you'll find many wildflowers in spring.

Trailhead: From US27, 11 miles south of Oneida and 4.6 miles north of Elgin, turn west on Mountain View Road; a sign says "Burnt Mill Bridge Access." At 1.4 miles, signs direct you right, then left, and at 3.6 miles at a four-way intersection, right on a dirt road. You can also reach this point if you are coming from the west on TN52; turn north a half mile before Elgin and go 3.3 miles to the four-way intersection and go straight ahead on the dirt road. Bear left in another half mile, and then in another 0.4 mile, you'll cross Burnt Mill Ford Bridge. Parking is on the left beside the river.

Description: To do the Burnt Mill Bridge Loop counterclockwise, walk across the road and watch for the blaze that marks the trail passing into the woods. The trail parallels the river downstream, crossing boardwalks that get you over marshy areas. Watch for side paths that give you access to the river. The cool forest and places for taking a dip in the river make this a trail to hike in the summer. Spring and early summer, the trail is thick with blooming rhododendron and laurel.

You'll soon pick up a rock wall on your left. The trail climbs slightly and then drops back to the edge of the river by a wooden stairway with no handrail. Stone steps take you under a rock overhang. Then at about 0.8 mile, the trail begins a climb away from the river.

Burnt Mill Bridge (courtesy of National Park Service, Bill Deane)

The trail crosses a creekbed on a wooden bridge and then joins an old jeep road. At about 1.1 miles, the trail takes a sharp left away from the road but then rejoins it soon after; watch for the trail blaze. At 1.3 miles, you'll reach the junction with a section of the John Muir Trail. A sign says Beaver Falls is in 2 miles. Beware if you hike this trail; it's easy to get lost. The trail is blazed for only the first half mile, and eventually it ties in with a maze of jeep trails. When we explored it, we never found Beaver Falls and were actually lost for about 15 minutes trying to find our way back.

Bear left to continue the loop, you'll cross the Burnt Mill Ford Road and encounter a sign that says the bridge is in 2.9 miles. You'll soon descend by switchbacks and rock steps through hemlock and rhododendron coves to join the river upstream from the bridge.

Again the river will be on your right with a rock wall on your left. Watch for several places to walk out on rocks that stand at the river's edge and places where you can easily go wading. If the weather is warm, you'll be ready for another dip. When the trail forks with a jeep road, bear right.

At about 3.5 miles, the trail opens to a waterfront campsite with steps that lead into the river. The river bottom is smooth rock, excellent for wading.

The trail from here is not so well marked; keep looking for the trail blaze when you encounter old jeep roads. You'll follow a jeep road out of the waterfront campsite. When the road forks, go right. The trail narrows but then joins another jeep road. At about 4 miles the trail comes to a three-way fork; take the middle one, and you'll soon be back at the trailhead parking. You can take one last dip under the Burnt Mill Ford Bridge. This is a popular swimming hole and also a favored putin for river runners. The ford that people used before the bridge was built got its name from the burning of a nearby grist mill on the river's east side.

22 Honey Creek Loop

5.5 miles
Difficult
Elevation change: 400 ft.
Cautions: Stream crossings, caged ladders,
boulder passages
Connections: None

Attractions: Honey Creek Pocket Wilderness was originally developed by the Southern Division of Bowater Incorporated but was included in the authorized boundaries of the BSFNRRA. The paper company had set aside the area because of its outstanding scenic attractions that include overlooks of the Big South Fork and numerous waterfalls and rockhouses.

Trailhead: Follow the directions in Trail #21 to the Burnt Mill Ford Bridge and continue up the hill past where the Burnt Mill Bridge Loop crosses the road. At 3.2 miles from the bridge, the road forks. Turn right 0.1 mile to a wide area in the road where you can park. The trailhead is just ahead on the right side of the road. The dirt road you are on continues to an overlook of the Big South Fork, but only four-wheel drive vehicles should try it.

Description: The trail first climbs a few feet and then passes through plateau forest before beginning the descent into a side canyon of the Big South Fork. You'll work your way down through small second-growth timber across a couple of footbridges and a stream and ascend to huge beech and hemlock trees as you walk along a hundred-foot rock wall.

At about 1.5 miles, a side trail leads up caged ladders to the canyon rim for panoramic views of the Big South Fork. At the top, take the right fork and walk along the canyon bluff. The trail soon forks; either way eventually rejoins the main trail. The left fork leads to the Honey Creek Overlook that you could have reached by continuing on the road where you found the trailhead.

The views from the top along this side trail make the climb well worth the effort, but you can skip the climb and continue straight ahead on the main trail. In just 0.2 mile, the side trail to the overlooks descends the wall of the canyon from the right and rejoins the main trail.

Continuing on the main trail, you'll reach a fork; you can go either way. The trail soon after makes its closest approach to the river. If you want to stand at the water's edge, you'll have to bushwhack your way down to the riverbank.

At about 1.8 miles, the trail turns away from the river and follows a creek upstream. This is Honey Creek, a small tributary of the Big South Fork. Along this section of the trail, you'll have a hard time making any headway. Every hundred yards or so you'll find a waterfall or rockhouse that must be explored as the trail passes between and sometimes under boulders. At several places, ribbons of water spill over rock overhangs into small pools wedged against cliff walls. You'll pass through small canyons, sometimes in the creekbed itself, making your way over rocks glazed with sheets of rushing water. In one close canyon, your choices are to walk in knee deep water, fight through the thick rhododendron on the right, or balance along a narrow rock shelf on the left.

The rockhouses are large and frequent. Usually the trail skirts the openings, but at 2.5 miles a fork to the right leads to a rockhouse several feet above the trail. A ladder up to the opening has been here a long time, but when we were last there it had about fallen apart. Take care if you try to use it.

At 3.1 miles the trail forks; go straight. Then at 3.4 miles you'll find Boulder House Falls pouring through an opening between massive boulders and giving a sheen to the rock floor beneath. At 3.6 miles the trail forks; go right. And again at 4.0 miles; go either way and cross a footbridge at 4.2 miles.

You'll encounter a side trail to the left at 4.3 miles that leads to Honey Creek Falls. The creek slips into a grotto and falls several feet into a deep green pool.

Retrace your steps to the main trail and continue. You'll make several crossings of an old logging road. Then toward the end of the loop, the trail makes a gradual climb and loops back to the parking area at the trailhead.

23 Gentlemen's Swimming Hole and Meeting of the Waters Loop

3.2 miles
Moderate
Elevation change: 200 ft.
Cautions: Steep climb
Connections: Bluff Trail

Attractions: Although outside the BSFNRRA, Rugby is an important historic attraction. On your visit, you can walk the loop trail to the swimming hole on the Clear Fork River and the confluence of White Oak Creek.

Trailhead: Historic Rugby is located 7 miles west of Elgin and 18 miles east of Jamestown on TN52. On the west side of the community, turn north on the Laurel Dale Cemetery Road. Continue straight to the cemetery where you'll find parking for the trailhead and a sign for the trail to the left.

Description: When the famous English writer Thomas Hughes visited Rugby in 1880, he awoke the first morning to the sounds of young men gathering. "In a few minutes," Hughes writes, "several appeared in flannel shirts and trousers, bound for one of the two rivers which run close by. . . . They had heard of a pool 10 feet deep . . . and a most delicious place it is, surrounded by great rocks, lying in a copse of rhododendrons, azaleas, and magnolias." The pool the young men were bound for was the Gentlemen's Swimming Hole.

To get to the swimming hole, follow the trail from the cemetery. After a short walk, you'll cross a creek and descend stone steps. The trail continues to drop while paralleling the creek cascading down the hillside. At half a mile, you'll reach the junction on the left with the Bluff Trail, a mile-long trail that began at the double gate you passed along the cemetery road.

Rugby House

Keep straight on the main trail until at 0.7 mile a second side trail to the left takes you down to the Clear Fork River and the Gentlemen's Swimming Hole. At the river's edge, a long rock juts into the water. It's easy to picture the Rugby boys taking a quick sprint along the top of the rock and a flying leap into the river.

From the swimming hole turnoff, continue on the main trail, which follows a rock bluff along the river's edge. At 1.7 miles, you'll reach the confluence of White Oak Creek and the Clear Fork River, the "Meeting of the Waters." The trail leads onto a broad slab of rock and then up White Oak Creek a short distance before making a steep climb and joining a logging road that leads back 1.5 miles to the cemetery.

The last English colony in the U.S., Rugby was founded by Thomas Hughes as a home for second sons of English nobility. Having no inheritance, second sons had no option other than joining a profession. They were free to make a living with their hands only if they relocated to another country. Hughes intended the Rugby community to support itself by farming. Unfortunately the colonists knew little about farming, and so the colony was never much of a success. The English investors sold out to American interests around the turn of the century.

The community stood in the solitude of the Cumberland Plateau until in the 1960s the Rugby Restoration Association was formed to preserve the homes and public buildings. Today, Rugby is on the National Register of Historic Places.

Of the fifteen original structures that remain in Rugby, several are open to the public. You can take tours of the community daily except during the winter months. Park near the center of the town next to the visitor center, which is located in the former schoolhouse, a two-story frame building constructed in 1907 after the original burned. Nearby Percy Cottage, which is used for offices, is a historic reconstruction of the original built in 1881 by Henry Kimber, a financial backer of the colony.

Adjacent to the visitor center parking area, you'll also find Kingston Lisle, built around 1884 as a summer home for Thomas Hughes. Across the road, stands Christ Church, Episcopal; the church opened in 1887 and is still being used for public worship.

Perhaps the most interesting building in Rugby is the 7,000-volume Thomas Hughes Public Library just east of the visitor center. As a tribute to Hughes, American and English publishers donated the books, which date from 1687 to 1899.

West of Kingston Lisle are three new buildings. The Board of Aid is a 1989 reconstruction of the original land office that was built in 1880 and burned in 1977. There's also the Commissary, which houses a craft and gift shop, and the Harrow Road Cafe, where you can get a meal.

You can find lodging at Newbury House, the colony's original boarding house that sits on Newbury Road behind the cafe. You can also stay at Pioneer Cottage, the first frame house in Rugby where many newcomers stayed while their homes where being built. Contact Historic Rugby, Inc., for reservations.

The remaining buildings in the community are private homes that are open to the public only during certain festival days. On the east end of town stands Roslyn, built in 1886 and named for Roslyn Castle in Scotland.

South of the center of town, several homes are located on a complex of dirt roads: Ingleside built in 1884, Adena Cottage and The Lindens built about 1880, and The Wren's Nest built in 1887. Along the Laurel Dale Cemetery Road, you'll find Martin's Roost, a reconstruction, and Oak Lodge that served as an overflow boarding house during the time of the colony. On the west end of town, there's Ruralia and Twin Oaks built about 1884.

On the west side of Rugby, you'll also see Uffington House on the north side of TN52. This residence was the home of Margaret Hughes, the mother of Thomas Hughes. Margaret Hughes believed in her son's dream of a new English colony and moved here from England in 1881. She was a central figure in the colony until her death in 1887. She is buried in the Laurel Dale Cemetery that rests near the beginning of the trail to the Gentlemen's Swimming Hole.

On your way to the trailhead, notice the open field on your left after turning on Laurel Dale Cemetery Road. This is where Rugby's Tabard Inn once stood. The original burned in 1884. It was rebuilt but burned again in 1900. You can still find foundation stones on the site. Plans for the BSFNRRA call for the reconstruction of Rugby's Tabard Inn as a lodge for the park.

24 Colditz Cove Loop

1.5 miles
Moderate
Elevation change: 100 ft.
Cautions: Steep descent, boulder passages
Connections: None

Attractions: Colditz Cove is a Tennessee State Natural Area near the southern border of the BSFNRRA. Because this is one of the loveliest spots on the Cumberland Plateau, you should combine this hike with your visit to Rugby. Big Branch drops 60 feet into Colditz Cove to form Northrup Falls, named for a family that once operated a water-powered sawmill that stood at the top of the waterfall. The falls ranges from a roaring cascade in wet weather to a whisper in drier seasons.

Trailhead: Colditz Cove is off TN52 11 miles west of Rugby and just east of Allardt. Turn south on the Crooked Creek Hunting Lodge Road. At the turn, you'll see a small sign to Colditz Cove, but more obvious is the sign directing you to Crooked Creek Lodge. In one mile along this road, Colditz Cove will be on your right, marked only by a sign and a parking area.

Description: From the parking area, follow an old jeep road that is now gated for about half a mile. As you walk through the scrub forest along the road, you'll wonder if this is going to be a waste of time. But almost as if walking through a door, the forest turns to a lush, green wonderland. Even in winter, the cove is green because of the profusion of hemlocks and rhododendron.

Just before the edge of the cove and a precarious view of Northrup Falls, a sign directs you left along the one-mile loop. You could also go right; at times when we have been here, the sign has been swiveled around to point right. But go left.

The trail passes along the bluff with a view of the falls and eventually drops into the cove; the descent is initially steep. The trail then doubles back along the base of the rock wall, moving over rocks and ducking behind a small waterfall formed by a spring before entering a long rockhouse that sweeps around to the main falls. The trail passes behind Northrup Falls and then begins the gradual ascent out of the cove to return you to the beginning of the loop.

The Colditz Cove State Natural Area is practically within the community of Allardt, which was originally a German colony founded about the same time as Rugby. While the English colony was a financial failure, the Germans who came from Michigan and directly from Germany to settle the town were successful in establishing a good financial base combining farming, lumbering, and coal mining. In spite of its success, the town never grew much beyond a busy intersection.

The architecture of the town is not as interesting as that of Rugby, which is probably why Rugby is so much better known. But you can still find here the small white building in the center of town that is the Gernt Office where the descendants of Bruno Gernt, who founded the community along with M. H. Allardt, still manage the family's holdings. The town was named for Allardt, who died just as the settlement began to form. East of the Gernt Office stands the abandoned Colditz Store that operated until 1962. It was the Colditz family that later donated land for the state natural area.

East off TN52 on a gravel road, you can visit the old Bruno Gernt House, a large gray farmhouse with brick-red trim which is on the National Historic Register. The house is available to the public as a bed and breakfast. This is a favorite place for us; we were married here in 1988.

Northrup Falls

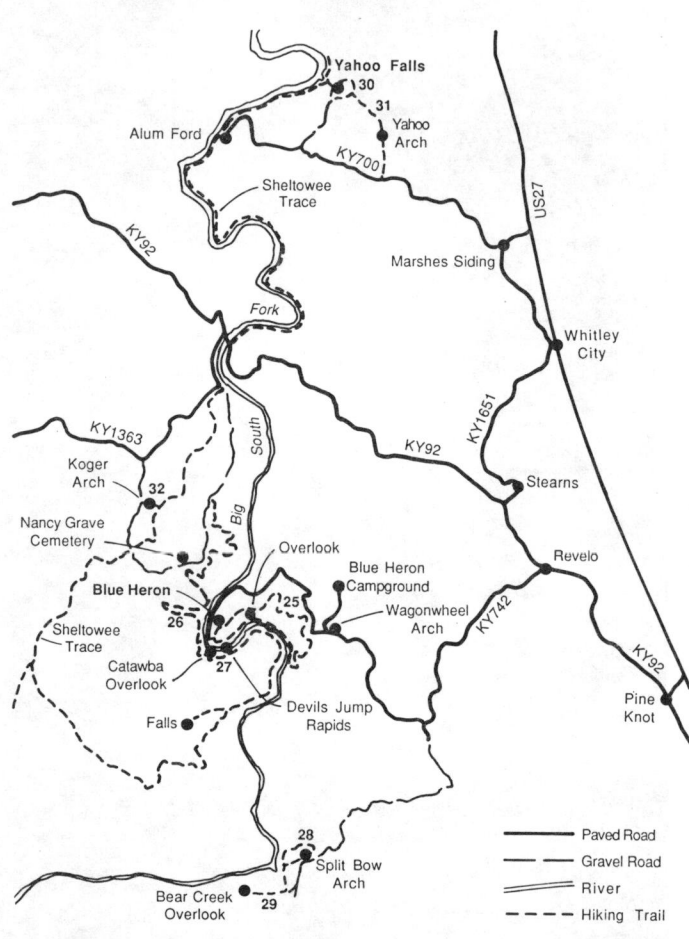

Blue Heron and Yahoo Falls

25 Blue Heron Loop

6.6 miles
Difficult
Elevation change: 400 ft.
Cautions: Boulder passages, steep stairs,
stream crossings
Connections: None

Attractions: Beginning at the Historic Blue Heron Mining Community and taking you through "Cracks in the Rock," this trail offers scenic views of the gorge and Devils Jump rapids.

Trailhead: On US27 between Oneida and Whitley City, turn west on KY92 in Pine Knot. At Revelo turn left onto KY742 and drive 9.2 miles to Blue Heron. Or to take the Big South Fork Scenic Railway to Blue Heron, continue straight at Revelo on KY92 for 1.1 miles to Stearns. The train departs the depot for Blue Heron at various times depending on the day of the week and the season; so you'll need to check the train's schedule beforehand for when you'll be in the area.

Description: From the exhibit parking lot at Blue Heron, one of several coal mining camps built and owned by the Stearns Coal and Lumber Company in the early 1900s, begin the loop at the top of the Mine 18 tipple. The tipple, a model of engineering technology, operated from 1937 to 1962 and at the time was the most advanced tipple on the southeastern coal fields.

The tipple stood alone as a reminder of the abandoned mining camp, until the recent reconstruction of "ghost" structures and the voices of those who once lived at Blue Heron joined to tell of life in a once bustling mining community. "Blue Heron" was actually a Stearns Company name for a particular grade of coal.

Walk clockwise past the mine-entrance exhibit behind the tipple. The trail soon leaves the pavement to cut back right and climb into the woods.

Cracks in the Rock

After two ascending switchbacks, you'll find yourself at 0.4 mile sandwiched between two monoliths as the trail narrows and stairs lead you up through a sandstone chamber. This is "Cracks in the Rock."

Climbing gradually, keep right when you encounter a side trail that will eventually lead to an overlook. At 1.0 mile, the trail parallels a road to your left. At 1.5 miles, you'll come to an overlook parking area. Walk to the overlook for a view of the gorge and the Devils Jump, a rapids in a narrow part of the river gorge.

Retracing your steps from the overlook, the trail turns off to the right into the woods before you get back to the parking area. From here, it climbs gradually, follows the roadside, and at 2.5 miles climbs up wooden stairs to the paved road. Turn right, but do not cross the road. Walk along the guardrail and then turn right back into the woods.

Working its way to the river, the trail descends through boulders and skirts rock shelves and at 4.6 miles comes to a side trail leading left 350 ft. to Laurel Branch. To continue on the loop, turn right and take the lower trail to the left along the roadbed. The upper trail is a horse trail. You'll walk through reclaimed strip mining areas and cross creeks orange from leached sulfur and iron oxide and join an old railroad bed paralleling the river down to your left.

At 6.2 miles, take steep steps down to a reclaimed field. This can be tricky. Follow the small arrows on the posts to switch back toward the river before heading into the woods on the lower side of a settling pond.

At 6.4 miles you will get a riverside view of Devils Jump rapids. Continue on and you'll soon reach the Blue Heron Exhibit Parking Area. Before the parking area, you can bear right to climb up to the powder magazine and complete the loop back to the tipple.

26 Old Tram Road

1.5 miles one way
Moderate
Elevation gain: 200 ft.
Cautions: Marshy areas, stream crossings,
boulder passages
Connections: Sheltowee Trace

Attractions: This trail follows the roadbed of an old electric tram once used to haul coal to the Blue Heron tipple.

Trailhead: Follow the directions in Trail #25 to Blue Heron.

Description: When the Blue Heron tipple was operating, small electric engines, hardly more than electric cars, pulled trams from the west side of the Big South Fork over the high tram bridge that still spans the river. The trams, open railway cars, were loaded with coal from several mines on that side of the river. The tram bridge to the tipple is now a footbridge that connects with the trails on the west side of the river.

From the top of the tipple above the Blue Heron parking area, take the tram bridge across the Big South Fork. At the end of the bridge turn right at the trailhead sign. You will now be following the old tram road that ran up and down the west side of the river.

After a short distance, the trail forks. Take the grassy trail up to your left. This part of the trail is marshy in rainy seasons. At about 0.5 mile, turn right and descend to cross Devils Creek. The trail then climbs to rejoin the old tram road where for half a mile or more utility poles and pipes protruding from a rock wall on the left remain as testimony to the tram railcars pulled by electric engines that once traveled this rocky ledge.

The tram road remains are the main attraction of this trail; so you can turn around and head back to the Blue Heron whenever you like. The trail does continue on and connect with the Sheltowee Trace National Recreation Trail in a total of 6.6 miles from Blue Heron.

Blue Heron Coal Tipple

27 Catawba Overlook and Big Spring Falls

3.4 miles one way
Moderate
Elevation gain: 350 ft.
Cautions: Stream crossings, steep stairs,
mudholes, poison ivy
Connections: Sheltowee Trace

Attractions: This trail climbs to a scenic view of the river from Catawba Overlook and then continues on to a waterfall in Big Spring Hollow.

Trailhead: Follow the directions in Trail #25 to Blue Heron.

Description: From the top of the tipple above the Blue Heron Parking Area, take the tram bridge across the Big South Fork. A sign at the end of the bridge directs you left 1.6 miles to the Catawba Overlook. As you begin your walk, you'll have to slog your way through a marshy area if there has been a recent rain. This trail south is the old tram road. The tram line hauled coal from mines on this side of the river across the bridge to the tipple. Watch for the abandoned "dump bottom" tram cars tipped over to the left of the trail. These cars had a 3-ton capacity.

At about 0.2 mile the trail forks. The left fork is closed. Take the upper trail to the right and continue along the old tram bed, crossing a short footbridge. You'll then bear left to Three West Hollow at about 0.4 mile. Cross the creek on a footbridge and switch back left. You'll climb from the creek, crossing three footbridges over wet weather streams until you reach a shear rock bluff on your right at 0.7 mile. Watch for wildflowers in spring: purple phacelia, stone crop, violets, foamflower. Continue walking along rock bluffs through a forest of mixed hardwoods and climb steep wooden stairs over a rock shelf lined with rhododendron.

At 0.9 mile the trail briefly joins a horse trail then turns left toward the bluff's edge through boulders and past American holly, laurel, rhododendron, and ground cedar.

Curve right into the woods and then back around to the canyon's edge and the Catawba Overlook, named for the Catawba rhododendron that blooms rose purple in May. A trail takes you down to your left to a platform reaching out over the river gorge.

At the overlook, you'll have a panoramic view of the Big South Fork Canyon. To the left you'll see the end of the Blue Heron Community and the tram bridge stretching across the river. On the opposite side of the river from Catawba, you'll see the Devils Jump Overlooks perched on the edge of the canyon and, to the right, Devils Jump roiling the surface of the river.

In the early years of the Big South Fork region, lumber was an important economic resource. Log rafts were floated downstream to mills in Kentucky. The men that road the log rafts were called "Devils." Presumably the rapids got its name when the devils jumped off their rafts and swam to shore at times when the water was too high to safely ride through the rapids.

From the Catawba Overlook, you can continue south, vaguely following the route of the old tram road to see a couple of waterfalls. The trail at times becomes a little overgrown because this continuation of the trail is seldom used; in places it's thick with poison ivy.

You'll cross another footbridge and at 1.9 miles join an old roadbed where you'll turn right and parallel an open area that was perhaps once a housesite. The trail drops into a cove and crosses a stream on a boardwalk. You'll ascend from the stream and find yourself once more on an old roadbed, but then bear left off the road.

At 2.1 miles, you'll use a set of wooden stairs to climb over a hemlock lying across the trail. The trail makers probably went to all the trouble of building the stile to preserve the tree that, although is prone, is still rooted to the ground and whose branches have grown straight up to become small trees themselves. Soon after, you'll descend a set of stairs down a bluff and bear left to Dick Gap Falls at 2.2 miles. The slender waterfall is off the trail to the left, and although you can see it from the trail, you'll have to bushwhack if you want to get near the falls because there is no path to it.

The trail bears right past the falls, and at 2.3 miles you'll join an old roadbed and switchback left. You'll hear a small stream to the right and then descend stone steps to cross the stream. You'll then see to the left where this side stream joins the stream that makes Dick Gap Falls.

As you continue down the old roadbed, the main stream cascades down a small gorge. You'll descend to a sign that says the way back is 2.0 miles, but in our judgment we had come about 2.6 miles. The sign is probably a leftover from when the trail to Catawba Overlook had been judged one mile instead of the actual 1.6 miles. At this junction, you'll bear right on what appears to be the old tram road again; watch for the small openings to a couple of coal mines on the right. These are probably very dangerous and should not be entered.

You'll cross several wet weather streams with now the Big South Fork on the left. At about 3.2 miles you'll encounter a creek cascading down on the right and crossing under the old roadbed through a rock passageway. An old road leads up to the right, following the cascading stream, but keep straight ahead.

At 3.3 miles, the trail crosses Big Spring Creek on a wooden bridge. Some old foundations can be seen on the left on the far side. You'll ascend to a T; the trail goes right while the left is unmarked. Then at 3.4 miles, as the trail switchbacks left, a side trail to the right leads to Big Spring Falls. You'll walk a boardwalk over a marshy area at the foot of a rock overhang on your way to the falls. The 60-foot waterfall spills halfway down to splash on a rock ledge before making its second drop into a pool at the base.

Retrace your steps to the main trail and then back to Blue Heron. If you're out for a long walk, you can continue on to Oil Well Branch in another 5.6 miles; you'll pass a horse trail on the right that loops back toward Catawba Overlook. From Oil Well Branch, you can turn right on a dirt road to connect with the Sheltowee Trace National Recreation Trail in another 2 miles.

28 Split Bow Arch Loop

0.7 mile
Easy
Elevation change: 100 ft.
Cautions: Rock steps, boulder passageway,
stream crossing
Connections: None

Attractions: This loop takes you through a slender arch in one of the most picturesque settings in the park.

Trailhead: Follow the directions toward Blue Heron in Trail #25. On KY742 watch for the Bear Creek Scenic Area sign, which is 3.1 miles from Revelo. Turn left. Continue on Bear Creek Road for 2.0 miles then bear right at the Scenic Area sign. Turn left in 0.3 mile at another Scenic Area sign. Drive 1.0 mile to the arch overlook just off the road to the right. Continue another 0.2 mile to a gravel turnaround. Park here to hike the loop.

Description: The Split Bow Arch Loop is the park's newest trail. When we first hiked the loop, it was still under construction. The work is now completed, and the trail is well marked.

To begin the loop, walk to the right, north, from the parking area and you'll find the trail leading down into the woods. The trail winds down rock steps to a junction. This is the loop part of the trail. Bear right to hike the loop counterclockwise. The trail ascends along rock walls and into a narrow passageway. You'll then come to Split Bow Arch, created by a hole in the rock wall on your left. The trail passes through the large, delicate arch.

Step down from the arch and turn right to begin a wide loop around to your left, crossing a stream on a plank walkway, then ascending through a hemlock and hardwood forest to complete the loop. At the junction, turn right to return to the parking area.

Split Bow Arch

29 Bear Creek Overlook

0.3 mile one way
Easy
Level
Cautions: High cliffs
Connections: None

Attractions: This short walk offers a panoramic view of the Big South Fork and the top of the Cumberland Plateau.

Trailhead: Follow the directions in Trail #28 to the trailhead for the Split Bow Arch Loop.

Description: There was no sign marking the overlook trail when we were last there, but it is easy to find. From the end of the turnaround a crushed rock trail leads through an abandoned field for about 0.2 mile then bears right into the woods.

Soon you will come to a platform overlook offering a view that has Angel Falls Overlook as its only competition for best view in the park. From the Bear Creek Overlook you get a sweeping view of the Big South Fork Canyon carved deeply into the plateau.

The original plans for the park called for a lodge to be built near this overlook, but the proposal is being reconsidered because of the lack of electric and water services and the poor road into the area. A proposed alternative is to build a lodge near the Devils Jump Overlooks, which can be reached by continuing on Mine 18 Road on the way to Blue Heron past the Bear Creek Scenic Area turnoff, past the Blue Heron Campground on the right, to the overlook road on the left.

30 Yahoo Falls Loop

0.7 mile
Moderate
Elevation change: 100 ft.
Cautions: High cliffs, steep stairs, stream crossing
Connections: Yahoo Arch, Cliff Side Loop, Cascade Loop

Attractions: You will walk under a massive roof of rock with a slender waterfall dropping off the edge 113 feet before splashing into a pool below.

Trailhead: South of Burnside, and just north of Whitley City on US27, turn west on KY700. Continue on KY700 through Marshes Siding and follow the signs approximately 4.5 miles to Yahoo Falls.

Description: Enter the woods at the trailhead sign at the far corner of the parking area. To walk the loop to Yahoo Falls, pronounced "Yea-hoe," you will actually walk the Topside Loop clockwise, following first blue then yellow arrows. When we last walked this maze of short trails, the trails had been renamed and marked with new blazes. This was sometimes confusing since blazes from past markings were visible as well.

As you begin the trail, watch for a caution sign on the left. A short side trail leads to an overlook of the beginnings of Lake Cumberland—water backed up from Wolf Creek Dam far downstream on the Cumberland River. Continue on the main trail until at 0.1 mile you come to a fork. Take the descending trail to the left.

Soon you will come to a metal structure of platforms and stairs dropping through a break in the laurel-covered rock bluff and landing in a forest of towering hemlock and hardwoods.

At 0.2 mile a side trail, the Cliffside Loop, leads off to the left. It joins the Sheltowee Trace going south a short distance then climbs up to the road just below the parking area.

Stay straight on the main trail. Just before the falls, you will encounter another side trail to the left. This is the Cascade Loop. If you take this trail, you'll cross Yahoo Creek on a bridge below the falls. This 0.2-mile trail is especially interesting because it leads through narrow passages and into a side creek on stepping stones, eventually passing the Roaring Rocks Cataract before rejoining the main trail on the other side of the falls. If you hike this trail, you'll reach a junction with a connector to the main trail soon after the bridge, turn left and then right to stay on the Cascade Loop.

If you do not take the Cascade loop, continue straight on the main trail to Yahoo Falls where the creek has cut deeply behind the waterfall to create a long rockhouse. Rock steps take you down to the pool fed by the stream spilling over the sandstone lip 113 feet above. In the freezing cold of winter, a mound of radiant blue-green ice called an "ice cone" forms beneath the falls.

Pass behind the falls and stay right when you encounter another side trail to the left. This side trail is another connector to the Sheltowee Trace.

At the next junction, you can take the left side trail a short distance down to Roaring Rocks Cataract. If you continue on this trail across the creek, you will be headed back west on the Cascade Loop. Instead, climb back to the main trail junction and switch back left up the hill to the Yahoo Arch junction. The arch is left 0.8 mile.

Stay straight at the arch junction along the main trail lined with pink and white rhododendron blossoms in late June. You'll have several overlooks of the waterfall and cross Yahoo Creek just above the falls as you complete the loop and return to the parking area.

31 Yahoo Arch Trail

1.2 miles one way
Moderate
Elevation gain: 200 ft.
Cautions: High cliffs, stream crossing
Connections: Yahoo Falls Loop

Attractions: Walk along the cliff's rim above Yahoo Falls to an arch stretching approximately 80 ft.

Trailhead: Follow the directions to Yahoo Falls in Trail #30.

Description: From the trailhead at the far corner of the parking area, follow the yellow arrows of the Topside Loop for 0.4 mile. This is the upper section of the Yahoo Falls Loop. At the Yahoo Arch junction, ascend right and at 0.7 mile you'll enter the Daniel Boone National Forest, skirting a creek below on your left.

At 1.2 miles, you'll approach the arch under a rock overhang dripping ribbons of water at your feet. Stone steps take you to the arch, a remaining layer of sandstone spared from the erosion that took the layers of rock above. You'll find a second small arch concealed to the left as you walk through the large opening.

From the arch, you can continue on the trail half a mile, where you will hit KY700.

Retrace the trail back toward the parking area, and when you encounter the Yahoo Falls Loop, you can turn right, following the yellow arrows below the falls. Another option is to turn right again after this loop junction, following the blue arrows of the Cascade Loop along the Yahoo Creek for 0.2 mile before it rejoins the Yahoo Falls Loop en route to the parking area.

32 Koger Arch Trail

0.3 mile one way
Easy
Elevation gain: 150 ft.
Cautions: Creek crossing
Connections: Sheltowee Trace

Attractions: This short walk leads to an impressive arch in the Daniel Boone National Forest just outside the western edge of the BSFNRRA.

Trailhead: From Stearns, take KY92 west 5.0 miles to the Yamacraw Bridge. Turn left just across the bridge onto KY1363; watch for the old railroad bridge on your left. Drive 2.4 miles and turn left onto a gravel road and cross a bridge. At 0.7 mile a sign on the left side of the road signals the trailhead.

Description: Steps take you down to and across a creek. The trail then switches back left and ascends, paralleling the road below on your left.

As you round the corner of a rock wall on your right, the arch appears. The mass of suspended stone, a clearance of approximately 15 feet and a span of about 100 feet, was apparently once a rockhouse, the back part having caved in.

Retrace your steps to the trailhead. Or, to join the Sheltowee Trace, continue on the trail through the arch and up the steps a quarter mile.

Addresses & Phone Numbers

Big South Fork National River and Recreation Area
P. O. Drawer 630
Oneida, Tennessee 37841
615/879-4890

Big South Fork Scenic Railway
P. O. Box 368
Stearns, Kentucky 42647
606/376-5330 or 1-800-462-5664

Bruno Gernt House
Estate of Bruno Gernt
Box 69
Allardt, Tennessee 38504
615/879-8517

Charit Creek Lodge
LeConte Lodge, Ltd.
P. O. Box 350
Gatlinburg, Tennessee 37738
615/430-HIKE

Historic Rugby, Inc.
P. O. Box 8
Rugby, Tennessee 37733
615/628-2441

Pickett State Rustic Park
P. O. Box 174
Jamestown, Tennessee 38556
615/879-5821

Other Books from Laurel Place

The South Cumberland and Fall Creek Falls
A hiker's guide to the South Cumberland Recreation Area and Fall Creek Falls State Park in Tennessee. $6.95

The Best of the Great Smoky Mountains
A hiker's guide to the Great Smoky Mountains National Park of Tennessee and North Carolina. $6.95 (available Fall 1990)

***Historic Knoxville*, Bicentennial Edition**
A walker's guide to the historic city center, parks, and neighborhoods of this Tennessee city. $7.95 (available Fall 1990)

Gift Order Form

Send check or money order to:
   Laurel Place
   P.O. Box 3001
   Norris, TN 37828

   Telephone
   615/494-8121

Title	Price	Quantity	Total
The Best of the BSF, 2nd Ed.	$6.95		
The Best of the GSM	$6.95		
The South Cum. and FCF	$6.95		
Historic Knoxville	$7.95		
		Subtotal	
	Tenn. residents add 7.75% sales tax		
		Shipping and handling*	
		Total enclosed	

*Add $1.15 for shipping/handling if ordering one book or for each book if separate mailing is requested. We pay for shipping/handling if more than one book is ordered and mailed in one shipment to the same the address.

Ship to _____

Address _____

_____

Items offered subject to availability. Prices subject to change without notice.